CHEERLEADERS®

#11

CHEATING

JENNIFER SARASIN

SCHOLASTIC INC.
New York Toronto London Auckland Sydney

ISBN 0-590-33816-1

12 11 10 9 8 7 6 5 4 3 2 1   11   5 6 7 8 9/8 0/9

Printed in the U.S.A.   01

CHEERLEADERS

CHEATING

CHEERLEADERS

CHAPTER 1

The Bijou Cinema in the village was packed. Tarenton wasn't exactly the most exciting place to spend a Saturday night, so when a new first-run movie came to town, it was a real event. The six cheerleaders of Tarenton High made it a date to go to all openings as a group, regardless of who they were involved, or not involved, with. And tonight was no exception.

"Hey, this dog was supposed to be another *Star Wars*," Pres Tilford grumbled, his handsome face a study in annoyance.

"It wasn't that bad," Nancy Goldstein shrugged. Her dark, lustrous hair blew in the cold night breeze, and she shivered, then quickly took the black beret she had in her pocket and jammed it on her head.

"Naw, it just didn't make it for me." Walt Manners put a well-muscled arm around his girl friend Olivia Evans' slim form. "The special effects weren't even special."

1

"I know what you mean," Angie Poletti agreed. "I've seen spaceships blown out of the sky with lasers a zillion times now." Angie didn't complain about a lot of things, but when she'd spent her hard-earned allowance on a bad movie, she was justifiably annoyed.

Mary Ellen Kirkwood was the only member of Tarenton High's cheerleading squad who didn't comment on the film. She was far too busy observing a group of kids in the far corner of the parking lot. Mary Ellen, a tall blonde with the beauty and ambition to become a high-fashion model, generally considered herself above petty high school gossip — except when it concerned her. But tonight, she was fascinated by the possibilities of what she saw right before her eyes.

"I just don't believe this," she murmured, shaking her lovely wheat-colored hair. Tonight it was hanging loose, secured only by a flower comb on one side. The cold didn't bother Mary Ellen nearly as much as appearing unfashionable did.

"What don't you believe?" Olivia turned toward the group across the way as Mary Ellen pointed.

"Who's that?" Walt squinted into the dark. Couples and other groups were straggling out of the theater now, and the night was filled with the sounds of kids and car horns and engines starting up. "I see Hank Vreewright," he commented, "and Dave Gates with him. Those two guys are always together."

"But look who's with them!" Mary Ellen couldn't believe how obtuse her friends were. "It's Ben Adamson. Why would he be hanging

2

around with guys from *our* basketball team? They even look sort of friendly."

Nancy flushed as Mary Ellen said the name she most dreaded hearing. Her red cheeks were not caused by the cold, but by the feelings of excitement and embarrassment that Ben's presence always caused. The brilliant captain of Garrison High's basketball team had been Nancy's Waterloo. She'd dated him for a few weeks against her better judgment, and then, feeling like a total traitor to her own school and her team, she had ended the relationship abruptly. Then Josh Breitman came into her life and, for a while, she'd forgotten about Ben — or told herself that she had. She and Josh had everything in common, including two sets of parents who had been determined to match them up for a year. She and Ben, on the other hand, had nothing at all in common. Nothing but pure, unmitigated passion. When they looked at each other, sparks flew.

She had not given Ben up without a thousand regrets. He was the sexiest guy she'd ever known, and his unusual offbeat looks still danced before her eyes on nights when she couldn't sleep. Nobody she'd dated before or since had moved her the way Ben had.

"Yeah, that *is* pretty weird," Pres commented, wandering away from the group to get a better look. "I could have sworn those guys smelled blood every time they got within radar range of each other."

"Maybe Ben resigned from the Garrison team," Angie ventured.

"Are you kidding? He's their pride and joy,"

3

Olivia scoffed. "They'd close down the school if he left."

"Well, they're gonna have to do just that," Walt Manners laughed, guiding Olivia toward his Jeep. Since they'd been an item, they never went anywhere without one another. It had seemed an odd pair at first — tiny Olivia with her dedication to hard work and discipline, with sturdy Walt, the class clown — but now everyone accepted their closeness.

"What are you talking about?" Nancy asked defensively. Somehow she sensed that he was going to give her an answer she didn't want to hear.

"Oh, it was a sad day at Garrison High, when Adamson said he had to fly," Walt sang in his off-key baritone.

"Walt, what do you know that we don't?" Mary Ellen demanded.

"Ben's transferring to Tarenton. And that's all I'm saying for now." Delighted to have an inside line on news that nobody else was privy to, Walt had decided to be mysterious, which certainly wasn't his style. No one was more open and willing to share than Walt Manners. The others looked after him curiously as he wisked Olivia off toward his Jeep.

The remaining four cheerleaders peered at one another in the darkness. Then, slowly, because there was nothing else they could learn tonight, they peeled off in separate directions, starting for their cars. Only Nancy remained rivetted in place, and her intent stare across the parking lot could have bored a hole right through the back of Ben Adamson's head.

The news was all over school the next day. Unbelievable as it sounded, the arch rival of Tarenton was now one of them. Ben Adamson, the whirling wonder of Garrison, the guy who'd taken the championship right out of Tarenton's grasp when he was only a junior, the person every Tarenton fan loved to hate — the *enemy* — was coming over to their side.

Nancy heard the Eismar twins talking about Ben during study hall, wondering whether there would be a place for him on the Tarenton team. Then, after math class, she passed Dave Gates in the hall, looking glum and grumbling to his pal Hank about being put on probation. Dave's grades had never been terrific, but now he was close to flunking out. "That rat's gonna get my position on the team if I'm benched," Nancy heard him say. She knew all too well who the rat in question had to be.

The last straw was Vanessa Barlow. When Nancy found herself on line in the cafeteria beside the daughter of Tarenton's superintendent of schools, she turned away quickly, hoping to get away unnoticed with her tuna sandwich and milk. But Vanessa had, of course, pushed her way up in the line in order to talk to Nancy, and avoiding her was like avoiding a bomber squadron intent on its search-and-destroy mission. The girl loved trouble, and Nancy could tell by the gleeful expression on her face that she was going to relish this unusual turn of events like nothing in recent memory.

"Well, I hear your boyfriend is finally going to be acceptable," Vanessa said, peering at Nancy from under heavily shadowed eyelids. A pair of expensive gold hoop earrings flashed next to her thick black hair, and to Nancy, they looked like warning beacons, cautioning her to stay clear.

"Oh?" She looked off into the line of pies, hoping to seem fascinated by the choice of cherry over blueberry.

"Of course, Ben Adamson probably had his fill of your company a long time ago. What a pity, now that you could date him without betraying your school and your team, that he'll be moving on to new territory! Seems to me that Mindy Norris is really his kind of girl, don't you think?" Vanessa gave a nasty little laugh and swept past Nancy and three other kids on line. The checkout cashier had long since given up criticizing her. After all, she could always get her father to fire him, so it was easier to ignore her bad behavior.

"Yeah, but what I don't understand is, What is Donny Parrish going to make of all this?" Pres was saying to his teammates. They were all sitting around a window table, eating and talking. "He's had it in for Ben for a year now."

"You're right — it's a problem. I mean, if Donny wasn't captain of the Tarenton Wolves, and if Ben hadn't been his opposite number at Garrison, maybe — just maybe, they'd learn to play ball together," Walt nodded, his mouth full of macaroni and cheese.

6

"I say they'll kill each other before they'll help each other score one basket." Olivia shook her head at Walt's atrocious table manners, then took a bite of her apple.

"I agree," Mary Ellen said. She had dated Donny for a while and knew just how fierce a grudge he held against Ben. "It'll never work. When's the wonder boy due to arrive on campus, anyway?"

"He's here already," Angie informed her.

"Oh, was that the guy you pointed out to me in the bookstore?" Arne Peterson asked her. Arne, a real brain who had been Angie's math tutor before they started dating, was not exactly up on school sports. As a matter of fact, if Angie hadn't practically dragged him to his first Tarenton game, he probably still wouldn't know the difference between a jump shot and a touchdown.

"That was Ben," Angie nodded. "We saw him today, big as life, at the back of the store with Mindy Norris and Susan Yardley, trying on Tarenton sweat shirts. The extra-large size just barely fit him."

Nancy, who had been standing apart, holding her tray close to her chest as if for support, suddenly had to sit down. Angie looked up at her and stopped talking, conscious of her friend's discomfort with the subject. "Sit down, why don't you?" she said in too cheery a voice, and then began chewing on the giant roast-beef hero that spilled over the sides of her plate. It wasn't hard for Angie to switch her attention when food was

7

involved. If only she could devise some way to remove all the calories from everything she put in her mouth, she'd be in heaven.

"All right, I give up." Mary Ellen turned to a very smug Walt with a pleading look on her face. "You said you knew why he's here."

Walt just grinned at her.

"C'mon, you! Tell! Otherwise I promise to kick your shoulder in that flying mount at practice this afternoon."

Walt looked around the table and smiled enigmatically. "What'll you give me for my info?" he demanded.

Olivia gave him a poke in the ribs. "That's what you get. I'm sure I know why Ben Adamson is at Tarenton. Big lummox was probably flunking out at Garrison and thought he could squeak by here."

"Well, he's *really* dumb if he thinks that," Mary Ellen scowled. "It's a lot harder at Tarenton."

"I know," Angie said decisively, looking up from her sandwich. "His parents must be after him to get a basketball scholarship to a great college. And everyone knows kids do a lot better, in terms of school placement, here than at Garrison."

"Well, if this guy thinks he's going to start scoring high in academics just because he's at a good school, he's got some *real* learning to do." Arne's piercing blue eyes stared at Angie intently from behind his glasses. "You still have to study to get good grades, no matter what."

"You guys are all wet." Pres shook his head knowledgeably. "Scouts for college teams pick players, period. They don't worry about which school they come from." His own father had been after him to get off the cheerleading squad and onto a team, ever since he could remember. It wasn't just that Preston Tilford II, one of the wealthiest men in town and the owner of Tarenton Fabricators, wanted Pres to continue the family tradition of going to Princeton. It was more that he couldn't stand the idea of his only son jumping around, as he put it, "like a jack-in-the-box." Pres had become a cheerleader precisely because it bugged his father.

"I wonder if it's the social life," Pres continued, leaning back far enough in his chair to topple right over. "Garrison is not blessed with too many foxy ladies, if I recall." He turned away from his friends, scanning the room for Vanessa. Actually, even though he was turned on by Vanessa and dated her when no one else was available, he didn't like the girl very much. She was just aching to make new conquests, which meant that she probably wouldn't leave Ben alone very long. Not that Pres really expected Vanessa to be the least bit faithful, but he didn't like the idea of her being interested in anyone else, either. Pres suffered from the typical rich-kid syndrome: He wanted things his way, and if he couldn't have that, then he didn't want them at all.

"You are all spinning your wheels," Walt looked directly at Nancy, who hadn't touched a thing on her tray. It was as if he was waiting for her to give them all the right answer. But at that moment, the group was interrupted by the sound of a hearty, deep, rumbling laugh. It was

9

Patrick Henley, draped from shoulder to knee with camera equipment. Mary Ellen looked up nervously at his approach.

"I've got the answer," Patrick stated, pulling the chair out from under Walt so that he could sit beside Mary Ellen. She glanced at him sideways from under her long, fair lashes, wishing he'd leave them alone — and praying he'd stay. She had this awful problem about Patrick, and it seemed to be getting worse. Although she longed to give in to his insistent wooing because she was terribly attracted to him, she couldn't get over the fact that Patrick was the son of Tarenton's trash collector, and always would be. He was actually proud of the fact that he had his own truck, and he boasted about expanding his father's business some day. How could Mary Ellen ever be satisfied with a guy who had his heart set on a life of garbage?

"And I will tell all," Patrick continued, "for one brief kiss from this fair damsel by my side."

His arm crept around Mary Ellen, who felt her limbs go numb with yearning. When Patrick was near her, the entire room seemed to melt away, and the people in it were so many motes of dust in the air. But she steeled herself against her feelings.

"Walt, it's up to you," Olivia insisted, her dark eyes keenly appraising her boyfriend's face. "I will make him tell," she assured the others. Olivia might be tiny, but she had an indomitable will that few could resist. After years of illness as a child, coming through one bout of heart surgery

10

after another, Olivia knew how to succeed at anything she put her mind to.

"Oh, all right," Walt said, pulling away as Olivia's small hands began pummeling his shoulders. "The reason that Ben Adamson is at Tarenton is because his parents just moved into a big house up on Fable Point, right near you, Pres. That means he's out of Garrison High's school district and in ours. My folks were doing some preliminary legwork for a show they're taping on the Tarenton real-estate boom, and they interviewed Mr. Adamson. According to Mom, who knows these things, the Adamsons' real-estate business really took off last year and Mrs. Adamson was pressuring her husband to buy over here. So they did."

The bell rang for the beginning of the fourth period, and the kids began picking up the remnant of half-eaten lunches and stacking their trays. They all noticed that Nancy had been completely silent throughout the whole conversation, but nobody dared to comment on it. It had to be hard for her, coming off a close relationship like the one she'd had with Josh and learning that this guy from her past was now going to become a fixture in her life. Because if Ben was at Tarenton, he was as good as on the basketball team, and if he was on the team, Nancy couldn't exactly *not* cheer for him. And if she cheered for him, what else might happen between them?

Nancy staggered through the rest of the afternoon with sweaty palms and a quickened pulse.

At each change of class, she wandered through the halls, certain that she would bump into Ben around the next corner. She saw him a hundred times, then realized she was staring at someone who looked nothing like him. What would she say to him if they did run into each other? "Welcome aboard," sounded dumb. like a *Love Boat* captain. "How've you been?" sounded too casual, as if she didn't care.

And she did care. Very much. Even though Ben hadn't come close to being the ideal boyfriend; even though, when they were dating. she'd always had the feeling he was parading her around like a trophy he'd won for a game wellplayed; she still couldn't shake off the need for him. Well, regardless of what she did or didn't do, she was going to have to talk to him sooner or later. Tarenton High wasn't big enough to stay out of anyone's way very long. What would be worse? she wondered, chewing on a pencil during study hall, just before practice: having him pursue her all over again or having him ignore her? She simply didn't know. She felt like an open wound, the edges sore and raw from Josh. And Ben was the container of salt, about to pour right in.

CHAPTER

"Not bad, Angie! Now get your leg up higher. Higher!" Ardith Engborg, the ball of fire who coached the Tarenton cheerleaders, was not taking no for an answer this afternoon. A petite, wiry woman in her mid-forties, Ardith was the spur that kept the kids going. She never slackened in her ambition to make this team the best — and to make the kids *want* to be the best. Sometimes her enthusiasm for the squad went beyond even their considerable abilities. But it was better to be pushed too far, as Mary Ellen always reminded the others. The fact that they all knew Ardith cared so much made them care, too.

"It doesn't go any higher than that, Mrs. Engborg," Angie smiled ruefully, her ankle resting lightly on Walt's shoulder.

"Well, work on it. Think of kicking the sky. Now Olivia, when you do that triple back flip, I want you to end up as close to Pres as you can.

Pretend you're going to step on his toes. You have to measure with your eye to see where you are after the second flip. Nancy, Mary Ellen, get the banana jumps in sync. Okay, start 'Let 'er Rip!'"

Ardith turned up her portable tape recorder, giving the squad a heavy dose of Michael Jackson's backbeat. The kids went into action, performing as though the few onlookers in the gym bleachers were a whole contingent of Tarenton fans, and they were on the verge of beating a rival team.

"Let 'er rip,
Get it going,
Don't be slow,
Make a showing!

"We're the ones,
Who can do it!
We're the team,
To get through it!
Tarenton's the Top!
Yay, team!"

Mary Ellen, captain of the squad, was in the midst of an "Around the World" with Pres when the doors to the gym opened and a group of laughing, yelling guys came running in, dribbling a couple of basketballs, passing them back and forth among themselves. It was unheard of for anyone to disturb cheerleading practice, and for a second, the six members of the squad stopped to see what the commotion was about. Only

Ardith's commanding voice made them go back to work.

"Don't pay any attention to that! What's wrong with you? I said, Keep going." She was clearly furious, and just barely managing to keep herself in check.

The squad moved mechanically through the next couple of cheers, and the basketball players were forced to keep their distance at the far end of the court. The noise level dropped as soon as they heard the tone of Ardith's voice.

But then the door opened again, this time for the basketball coach, Mr. Cooley. He was followed by a group of reporters from the school paper, and Patrick Henley, the official Tarenton photographer, with all his camera equipment. On seeing them, Ardith sighed and snapped off the tape recorder. She clapped her hands, bringing the cheerleaders to a dead halt.

"I'm afraid I forgot that I promised Mr. Cooley he could use the gym for pictures this afternoon. I'm letting you off early, but only on the condition that you make some time for yourselves this weekend to work on the new routines that Walt and Olivia came up with. Thank you, that's all for today," she dismissed them curtly. Then, with a menacing glance at the basketball coach, the photographer, and the reporters, she stalked out of the gym.

Nancy was dizzy, and it had nothing to do with the fact that she'd been standing on her hands a minute ago. *He* had just walked into the gym, and the blood had rushed to her cheeks. Yes, he looked just the same, that angular hawklike face, with the prominent cheekbones and deep-set dark eyes. His broad shoulders made him appear even taller than he was, even more imposing. His dark shock of hair was unruly, a little too long in back. He moved around the court like he owned it, and the other boys stood out of his way. Ben Adamson had already claimed a space at Tarenton, there was no question about that.

"Can I get those pictures of the team now, Mr. Cooley?" Patrick Henley asked. "I want some head shots, and then some action — the guys dunking a few, how's that?"

"Sounds good, yeah. Why don't you let the team warm up a little first. Donny, you and Ben tip off. Adamson, don't get all hot under the collar — you're on hold. Not on the team till I say so, right?"

Walt and Olivia exchanged glances as they watched the beefy, balding coach lining the guys up.

"Right, Mr. Cooley." Ben's smile indicated that he didn't feel he was in much danger of being asked to sit on the sidelines. If he wanted to be on the Tarenton team, he would be.

The team split in two for the practice, and the star centers moved into position. All eyes in the gym were on Ben Adamson as the coach threw the basketball high in the air. All, that is, except Mary Ellen's. It was almost as if the sight of these boys grabbing for position and power made her realize where the *real* values lay. The one person in the room who didn't seem to have to prove himself was Patrick Henley. He had a job to do, he enjoyed doing it, and he didn't have to show off to make his presence felt.

Patrick had something that none of those other boys had. All that scrabbling to impress, all those wise-alecky remarks and high jumps were kid stuff. Patrick had class; he knew who he was and he was proud of it, and every time she saw him next to one of his immature classmates, she was once again bowled over by his extraordinary self-confidence and ease.

As the others cheered the Varsity basketball players, Mary Ellen found herself totally pre-occupied with Patrick, and mad at herself for being so. After all, as cheerleading captain, she was practically responsible for mustering school spirit. She should be as concerned with the possibilities of a new player on the Tarenton team as the coach was himself. Instead, all she could think about was Patrick's hands, steadying the Nikon; Patrick's graceful body, moving around the court for the best angles; Patrick's mouth, so often curved into the most seductive smile imaginable.

"This I gotta see." Pres took Mary Ellen by the hand and dragged her over to the nearest bench. "Donny and Ben together." He put a hand to his heart and sighed in mock romantic despair. "Will the two team captains be reconciled at long last? Will they bury their hatchets and play as one? Or will the terrible vendetta continue? Tune in next week and — "

"Oh, shut up, Pres," Nancy barked at him, and when he saw the look on her face, he was silent immediately. He liked Nancy, and respected

17

her for the choices she made. Not to mention the fact that he found her terribly attractive. He'd never dated Nancy, and didn't have any intention of doing so because he felt they were too different to really link up, but he understood where she was coming from. Having been involved seriously with someone himself — adorable, lovely Kerry Elliott — and having had it come to an abrupt end, he could understand how Nancy must feel about Ben.

"Let's go!" Coach Cooley blew the whistle and the practice began in earnest. Ben tipped the ball to his side and was on top of it immediately, scarcely giving his teammates a chance to get it closer to the basket. Hank caught it on one bounce, passed it to Chuck Maxwell, who gave it back to Ben. He dribbled once before tossing it casually from the back court. It rimmed the hoop, then dropped in.

"The guy's dynamite. What did I tell you?" Walt was on his feet, pacing, watching the action eagerly. When Ben scored a third time in a row, Walt let forth with a "Go, Adamson!" and a stag leap.

Olivia couldn't contain herself either. She was hopping excitedly from one foot to the other, punctuating her dance with little stabbing thrusts of her fists. "Get 'em! That's it, Ben. Don't give that nerd the edge. Dunk it!" She muttered her encouragement like a prize fighter's manager, determined to see his man win.

Angie had joined Nancy on the bottom row of the bleachers, scarcely taking her eyes off the wild action on the court. "Wow, is he good! Tarenton can't lose a game with Ben on the team. If only he would just stop trying to get the best of Donny."

Patrick, who was standing in front of the girls, aiming and shooting, nodded his head without turning around. "A love-hate relationship. It's the pits." As he lowered his camera briefly, his eyes met Mary Ellen's across the court, and the other two girls knew he was thinking about his own conflicts with their stubborn, unreachable squad captain. Mary Ellen loved Patrick, and hated the fact that she loved him. But as he looked her way, he found her staring back, just as he knew she would be. "Wait for me afterward?" he mouthed. He caught the vehement shake of her head, but he just smiled at it. He knew she'd wait.

Everyone else in the room was busy watching the clear competition between Donny Parrish and Ben Adamson. Now, as the two boys played furiously, going for reverse lay-ups and hook shots one after the other, it seemed hard to believe that they could work together toward any goal. Then Chuck Maxwell fouled Dave Gates, and the coach blew his whistle. "Want some pictures of a free throw, Henley?" Mr. Cooley asked.

"No thanks. Just the head shots and I'm through. I don't need any more after that hot action," Patrick said. His main reason for finishing up quickly was Mary Ellen. If he worked too long, she might vanish. He saw her as Cinderella, always about to escape out the door, her glass slipper flying off for him to catch. The only problem was, it was *his* carriage that was the pumpkin, not hers. His garbage truck was not her choice of vehicle, not by any stretch of the imagination.

Ben, now dripping with perspiration, grabbed the towel he'd left on the bench and draped it around his muscular neck. But instead of walking over to Patrick to get his picture taken, he went directly to Nancy. She saw him coming and wanted to move, to run away quickly, to grab Angie's hand and head for the lockers. But she did no such thing. She sat completely still, listening to the sound of his rubber soles squeaking on the hardwood floor, counting the steps until he was by her side.

"Hiya, Nancy."

She remembered that voice. She remembered the raspy grate of it when he first spoke to her in the dark, when they felt their way down the corridor to the soda machine together, holding hands because neither of them could see a thing.

"Hi, Ben."

"Been a long time. But I guess we'll be seeing a lot of each other from now on. Now that I'm. . . ." He didn't bother to finish the sentence. He didn't have to. She was breathing as hard as he was, and she hadn't been running all over the court after a stupid basketball. She lifted her eyes slightly, grazing them along his chest. There was a dark wet spot right in the middle, and she could see the curling black hair through his thin cotton jersey. The sight made her fingers tingle, as though they wanted to reach out and touch the spot despite anything she might do to control them.

"I need a shower. But I don't have anything

after that. Want to go get a Coke?" He was grinning, aware of her reaction to him.

"I, uh. . . . Well, I really have a few things to do. Maybe some other time." She was trying to be strong.

Ben knelt down beside her, and his face swam into view before her eyes. He was smiling, a funny lopsided smile that put crinkles around the corners of his mouth. She noticed that he only had one dimple, somewhere back in his right cheek. She'd never noticed that before. "Nancy," he said, taking her hand, "there may not be some other time. The world could end tonight. How about it?"

"Okay," she answered breathlessly. She still hadn't moved, so he pulled her up beside him and started to walk her toward the lockers.

They were halfway across the court when Patrick ran up in front of them. "Just a second, Adamson. You don't escape that easy." He came in close to get a head shot of Ben. Patrick was tall, but he still had to aim up.

"Hey, I don't even know if I'm on the team yet," Ben shrugged with false modesty.

Patrick grinned. "What about it, Coach?" he called to Mr. Cooney. "Is Adamson in or out?"

Mr. Cooney gave the thumbs up sign. "If I didn't take him, I'd be outta my head," was his only comment.

"Then I get to pick my shots," Ben said, sweeping Nancy under his arm. "Here, Henley. Here's your picture." As Patrick looked down into his lens, he saw framed in his sights a very passionate kiss. Ben and Nancy, entwined in each other's arms, both of them clearly very happy about it.

"Okay, that's a wrap," Patrick sighed, snapping the cap back on his lens. Quickly, he gathered his equipment, and was out the door of the gym just as Mary Ellen disappeared into the girls' locker room. He glanced at his watch. She always took at least twenty minutes, usually more. That gave him plenty of time to stow his gear in the photo lab and meet her at the front door.

The object of his very intense interest was at that moment peeling off her practice clothes, considering her options. Mary Ellen was shrewd, and she was tough, but she wasn't always in control of her emotions. So when she saw Nancy wandering into the locker room in a daze, she sympathized. She'd been there herself.

"I take it you're going out with him," Olivia said. She was beet-red from the hottest shower she could tolerate, and her delicate face looked like she'd scrubbed it within an inch of its fresh appeal.

"Don't bother her now, Livvy," Angie smiled, wrapping her sopping hair in a towel. "She's in dreamland."

"You two leave her alone," Mary Ellen said defensively. "There are certain moments that have to be digested quietly, seriously."

"All I want to digest right now is a double cheeseburger with bacon," Angie said, somewhat apologetically. "Honestly, it's impossible for me to even think about romance after strenuous practice. All I've got on my mind is food."

"So what else is new?" Olivia shook her head disparagingly. She herself ate like a bird, despite her mother's best efforts to build up her strength with vitamin and mineral-packed meals. "C'mon, Angie. These two are not on our wavelength right now."

As Mary Ellen wandered slowly out the door of the locker room several minutes later, she had to acknowledge that Livvy was right. There were times when her head was clear enough to function normally, to think about schoolwork and the game on Saturday night and picking up her little sister Gemma. But there were other times when her brain was occupied, processing information about one set of sexy eyes, one powerful back, one pair of muscular legs. She was going through one of those times right now. Patrick Henley was never somebody she wanted to think about — but she just couldn't help it.

"Right on time," she heard him say.

Boy, Mary Ellen, she thought angrily, you're really a case. Now you're hearing things. But as she walked through the open doors of Tarenton High, she realized that Patrick was holding them for her. He stuck his head around the doorframe and bent it slightly, just to her level. Their lips were inches apart.

"Patrick. . . ." She was hot and cold all at once, and she didn't even feel the light raindrops of the winter evening landing on her upturned face.

"You look like you need a ride home. Or maybe a ride somewhere else. Your wish is my command," he added gallantly, as he took her old, frayed duffle bag with her practice clothes and slung it over his shoulder.

"Patrick, it's awfully nice of you. . . ." she began.

"Yes, it certainly is. So get in that truck before I turn not so nice and have to throw you in." His voice suggested all kinds of wonderful things she could never resist. Although there were times when his garbage truck repelled her, tonight was not one of them.

She climbed up inside without a word of protest, and he didn't question her eagerness. Patrick knew enough to take advantage of the edge he had over her. Mary Ellen might go for rides in Pres's fancy red Porsche, she might fool around with Donny Parrish because he was a Big Man on Campus and therefore worthy of her consideration, but she always came back to him. And even if it was only for a little while, he wanted it — wanted her. Because every time he was near her, he felt something he could only define as love. And every time she melted in his arms, he fooled himself into believing that it would be forever.

"Well, how do you like that," he sighed when they were both seated thigh by thigh in the cab.

"Like what?" she asked.

"Oh, everything," Patrick shrugged noncommittally. "That sliver of a new moon over there, for one. Ben and Nancy, for another. And you and me. Especially you and me."

As he leaned closer to claim a kiss, Mary Ellen efficiently clicked off her mind. She didn't like it to be working when she kissed Patrick, because it warned her, all the time she was enjoying herself, that she was making a big mistake. Tonight, she didn't need warnings. All she needed was him.

CHAPTER

It was a Thursday night, two days after the coach had officially put Ben on the team, that he came by for Nancy.

"Hey, glad you're home!" he said when she answered the doorbell. She'd watched out the window as he swaggered up her front steps like he owned the place. When she opened the door for him, he took her hands in his and held them, letting the warmth of his great huge paws cover her like a mantle. There was no reason to touch as much as Ben did, none except that he was a very physical person. Why shouldn't he touch her? The look in his eyes said that this time he intended to stick with their relationship.

"Aren't you going to ask me in to meet your folks?" he grinned.

She gave him a skeptical grin. "You never wanted to before."

"That was before I was Tarenton," he whis-

25

pered. "I'm a new man now. Much nicer. *Much* more interesting. Give me a chance, Nance. What do you say, hey?"

She giggled at his rhymes and led him into the living room, where her father was sitting reading the paper, his pipe jammed into a corner of his mouth. Knowing how crazy her parents had been about Josh, their best friends' son, she doubted that she was going to get a seal of approval on Ben. But suddenly, before she knew what was happening, Ben had her father going on about cars, and then her mother walked in and joined them, offering coffee and cookies. Nancy watched what was going on with both amusement and anxiety. There was something wrong here. She'd practically just broken up with Josh. She should need time to get over him. Her parents should need time to get over him, for heaven's sake! And, yet, here they all were, chatting happily as if it were the most natural thing in the world. By the time Ben had swept her out of the living room, down the drive to his brand new Isuzu, everybody was suspiciously chummy. What did it all mean?

All night, he looked for openings with her. He took her to the mall and bought her fries and Cokes.

"I love these things. Delicious, like you." She blushed as he took a French fry out of its cone and offered it to her, watching her eat it from his fingers. Then he linked his arm through hers, passing the cups of Coke in a lover's knot, so that she took sips under the shadow of his dark eyes. Later on, when they wandered out into the night and came to a slick patch of ice in the parking

26

lot, he literally swept her off her feet, carrying her, protesting and laughing, to his car.

"What are you doing? Put me down, Ben!" she insisted, not really wanting him to.

"I'm making myself indispensible. You can't make a move without me," he said with a wink, his craggy face smiling down at her. "Promise me you won't."

She hesitated, not knowing what to say. It was as if he was offering an invitation to stay with him; as if, this time, he wanted something permanent. And this time, Nancy was ready for it.

"Okay," she agreed breathlessly, just before he bent his head toward hers and kissed her. She closed her eyes and waited for the pounding of her heart to stop, but it refused to do so. The kiss went on a moment longer, as Ben's hands lowered her to the ground, then drew her close to him. She could barely hear the small voice in the back of her head telling her to take her time and watch out. But she didn't like the message at all, so she turned it off.

Angie watched Mr. Demerest handing out papers in fifth period civics class. She saw him walk down one row, grin, and deposit an essay, branded with a red "A," on Mary Ellen's desk. Then he sauntered up the next row and, with a disparaging shake of his head, place a "C-plus" essay in front of Vanessa. Arne, of course, had an "A-plus." She didn't even have to look over at him to know that. His studious face broke into a grin as he saw the mark, then quickly sobered again.

27

Pres's paper came down before him without any expression at all crossing the teacher's face. Pres so often botched up his grades, nobody was surprised. Then, the night before an important exam, he'd study himself into the floor and come up smelling like roses. At least he had while he was going with Kerry Elliot. It remained to be seen whether he'd have the same self-discipline now that Kerry was out of the picture.

Angie screwed her eyes shut as her own paper was placed before her. This was not going to be good news.

"I'm disappointed in you, Angie," Mr. Demerest said. "You were doing well for a while. But," he went on, turning to Nancy, who was sitting on the other side of the aisle, "I am astounded at your performance, Miss Goldstein. You have never done so poorly. To what, may I ask, can we attribute this execrable writing?"

There was silence, except for a few murmurs of kids asking one another what *execrable* meant. Then, from the hush, came Vanessa's clear voice.

"Not to *what*," she smirked. "To *whom*."

Nancy whipped around in her seat, knocking her notebook to the floor. The look on her face would have melted most loud mouths into a puddle of embarrassment. Not so Vanessa. She had the audacity to ask Mr. Demerest if she could submit a speech for the civics assembly at the end of the month. Nancy had practically been assigned that speech, since everyone acknowledged she was the best in the class.

Mr. Demerest took one look at his fallen

paragon and shrugged before turning to Vanessa. "You may as well try," he agreed. "If I don't see some improvement from this young woman," he nodded at Nancy, "the speech is up for grabs."

Angie was horrified, and told Nancy so as soon as the bell had rung and they were walking briskly down the corridor to study hall. "You can't let her snatch that speech away from you," she stated firmly. "I won't let you."

"It's not such a big deal, Ange."

Angie shook her head. Her fellow cheerleader was wearing that spacey look again, the one she'd had on her face since Ben Adamson had started at Tarenton. "It most certainly *is* a big deal. You're a brain, not to mention a terrific cheerleader. And now, just because of this . . . this person, you're a basket case. No pun intended."

But it had passed right over Nancy's head. She was, in fact, so preoccupied with Ben that it was difficult for her to concentrate, even at practice. Their dates were magical, filled with the kind of romance she'd been missing in her relationship with Josh. Josh was. . . . Well, he could aptly be described as the boy next door. He was easy to be with, full of fun, a good listener, a person with principles. Ben, on the other hand, was danger and excitement. He boasted a lot, flirted instead of talked, he drove a little too fast, and he took every opportunity to make physical contact with her. Sometimes he made her extremely nervous, though she couldn't put her finger on the reason for her anxieties. When he was at Garrison and they were going out on the sly, she'd been aware that he had a roving eye, that she was sometimes there with him as an afterthought. This time, though, he was determined. He wanted her around a lot, and he let her know in no uncertain terms that nobody else would do.

They had begun dating again without really talking about it, without even discussing the reasons why their relationship had ended the first time. Ben would casually come by for her after dinner, and he actually came inside to meet her parents each time. Then, as if it had just occurred to him, he'd say, What about hanging out at the mall for a while? or, Feel like a movie tonight? Nothing as set or formal as, Are you free next Friday? Ben called all the shots.

"You ought to put your foot down, you know," Olivia told Nancy in the locker room the night before the Tarenton-Northfield game. Their practice had been exhilarating, special. This would be the first time Ben would be playing on the team, and there was an air of expectation around the whole school. The cheerleaders could taste a win, and they were up for a great game.

"Where am I supposed to put that foot?" Nancy smiled as she looked at herself in the mirror. She really felt wonderful these days, and her dark, exotic good looks seemed touched with a new glow. As she gave her shining brown hair a final brushing, she couldn't help but feel on top of everything.

"Don't bother her about this," Mary Ellen cautioned Olivia. "It's not your problem whether Ben actually calls or just shows up."

"That's right," Nancy nodded, pulling on her high brown leather boots. He was waiting for her in the parking lot — he hadn't actually said he would be, but she felt it — she just knew it.

"Nancy, for heaven's sake. You never would have said that a month ago. How come you've let this doofus turn your brain to mush? You used to stand up for yourself," Angie said. She came over to the bench where the other three girls were putting the final touches on their hair and makeup. Nancy didn't look at her, didn't even acknowledge her statement.

"I hate to say this, but Ben and Nancy may be a problem that affects all of us, folks," Angie continued. "Nancy, I'm not criticizing or anything, but you were kind of shaky in the pyramid tonight. And your cartwheel circle ended up off-center."

"Now that you mention it," Mary Ellen acknowledged grudgingly, "you may be right, Ange. Didn't you stumble against Walt when you came down from that thigh stand, Nancy?"

"Listen." Nancy stood up, gathering her things quickly. "I'm sorry if you're all jealous. I don't think you've gotten over the fact that Ben is one of us now, that it's okay for me to date him. And I don't think any of you is really ready to congratulate me. So, if you'll excuse me, I think I'll just bow out of this conversation. And don't worry," she said as she reached the door of the locker room, "I'm not going to let the squad down — ever. I'll be fine at the game tomorrow night."

But as she ran outside into the clear, fresh air that held the promise of snow, she doubted her

31

own words. Ben's presence acted like a particularly potent drug on her. When she was flying high, she could do anything. When she was waiting around for him, she was a total wreck, incapable of tying her own shoelaces. This part of the dating relationship was something she couldn't share with the girls. And she disliked herself for responding to Ben as she did.

The entire school was pumped up for the game the following night. It was a home game, and this gave everyone ample opportunity to give their all for Tarenton. A committee of sophomores decorated the front doors and draped the bleachers with crimson and white banners. Patrick got a group of the newspaper staff together, and they sat around during the afternoon blowing up red and white balloons, to be released at the precise moment of the Tarenton victory. The cheerleaders themselves pitched in on the balloons, until Ardith came over to warn them about wearing themselves out.

"You guys need every breath you've got for the cheers," their coach scolded. "I'd rather see you get a little more practice before game time. What about it?"

So they practiced some more. They worked out diligently until five-thirty, at which point, Mary Ellen called a halt. The game would start at eight, and she wanted her squad rested before the main event.

But going home for dinner was anguish to all of them. Not only were they not hungry (except for Angie, who was hungry all the time), but the hours away from school and from one another seemed to wear badly on them. They were all in the locker room, dressed and ready to warm up, by seven-thirty.

"So we'll start with the name cheers and move on to Olivia's solo routine before the game," Mary Ellen reminded them. She looked lovely tonight, her blonde hair sweeping around her shoulders in delicate curls and waves.

Angie straightened the white pleats that peeked out of her crimson skirt. "We don't have a chance of losing, do we?"

"Are you kidding?" Walt exclaimed, turning down the turtleneck collar of his white sweater with the red "T" emblazoned on the front. "With Adamson on the team?"

"When Adamson gets the ball," Pres intoned with the practiced jargon of a sportscaster, "the next stop is the hoop. You will see a new page written in the history of Tarenton basketball tonight, ladies and gents."

"I certainly hope so," Olivia sighed. "The only problem is that Donny Parrish is still captain. I didn't think Ben could stand not being the person in charge. He's not exactly the type to let somebody else order him around."

She looked over at Nancy, who was on the floor, stretching her head to her knees. "How're you feeling, Nancy?" she asked solicitously. Of all of them, Olivia was least likely to ask this question, since she so resented her mother asking it of her all the time. Since her childhood illness, her mother had never been convinced that she was physically able to cross a street by herself, and even now, seeing Olivia flying through the air at games gave Mrs. Evans heart palpitations. But Olivia cared about Nancy, and she worried about her mood these days. So she had to ask.

"I'm perfectly fine," Nancy said with a sigh of exasperation. "Why do you all treat me like I'm infected with some awful disease?"

"Because you are," Walt pointed out cheerily. "Dry rot of the heart and mind. Whew, when Livvy fell in love with me, at least she was functional."

"Are you implying I'm not?" Nancy demanded, scrambling to her feet.

But there was no time for anyone to answer, because Ardith dashed into the room to inform them that the gym was packed to the rafters and the crowd was about to eat the bleachers if the game didn't start at once.

"Everybody's out there," Ardith told them. "Lots of Garrison kids, too. Guess they all want to scout out the competition and see how badly they're going to lose when it's their turn. Even Johnny Bainbridge, their new captain, showed up. So let's show them, okay? Give it everything you've got, and then some more!" their coach encouraged them as she pushed them out the door.

They hit the gym floor like six explosions, one right after the other. With a startling series of handsprings and pikes, the cheerleaders started their first cheers, causing even more commotion in the stands. Mary Ellen could see Patrick snapping away as she cartwheeled right into Pres's waiting arms and he picked her up from a backbend.

"We got the T-E-A-M
That's on the B-E-A-M!
We got the team that's on the beam
That's really gonna survive,
So c'mon, Tarenton,
Skin 'em alive!"

Tarenton proceeded to do just that. Donny tipped off with the Northfield captain, but as soon as the ball was in play, Ben was all over it. He consistently eluded his defense, wearing a grin that seemed to infuriate Northfield. He dribbled the ball as though he were taunting his opponents to take it away from him, then tried effortlessly for the sky hook that brought the crowd to its feet. A quick play followed where Andrew Polletti, Angie's younger brother, nearly lost the ball to a Northfield guard. But Ben recovered it, then raced downcourt for a neat lay-up. He was all over the place, scarcely giving his teammates a chance to score. He was the whole game, all by himself.

When Tarenton won, 56–24, nobody was surprised. And Nancy jumped higher and landed more gracefully than she ever had before. She was nearly bursting with pride for her school, her team, her guy. She had tears in her eyes as the referee announced the final score and the cheerleaders took the floor for their last display.

The exhilaration everyone felt was palpable in the room. Even after the cheerleaders had run out, following their brilliantly triumphant team, the crowd continued to laugh and exchange slaps on the back. And the excitement was still going on when the girls, now showered and changed, left the locker room.

"I have to find Walt. We're going out to celebrate," Olivia crowed, tossing her still-damp light brown hair.

"I'm going out for pizza with Arne and my brothers," Angie said. "Want to come, Melon?"

Mary Ellen's eyes darted hopefully into the waiting crowd. There was Patrick, still snapping pictures, and Vanessa beside him, posing. "I, uh . . . maybe I'll join you later, Ange," she said.

Nancy was waiting, with shining eyes, by the door to the guys' locker room. She and Ben hadn't discussed the evening ahead, but then, they didn't have to. She knew they'd be spending it together. As the door opened, she turned hopefully, but it was Pres.

"Oh, it's you," she said with less than her customary enthusiasm.

"Well, excuse me for living," Pres mugged. "As if I didn't know who you were waiting for. Hey, Vanessa, how'd you like the game?" he called, moving away from Nancy.

"Oh, it was all right," she shrugged. Vanessa was with a very solemn-looking Dave Gates, who had formally been tossed off the Tarenton team and who had watched tonight's game like a condemned man being served his last meal. Even Johnny Bainbridge, the Garrison captain, seemed more enthusiastic than Dave. Johnny had been flirting shamelessly with Vanessa before Pres's appearance. After all, there was precedent for a Tarenton girl to date a Garrison boy. But

Vanessa didn't seem all that interested.

"All right!" Pres shook his head in amazement. "It was spectacular. Adamson carried the thing on his shoulders all the way."

"But there was no competition," Johnny Bainbridge offered. "Just wait till you guys have to play Garrison," he went on with a leer in Vanessa's direction. "Then we'll see who's got the real stuff."

"He's probably right, Pres," Vanessa smiled, flipping her ebony hair over the collar of her classy antique raccoon coat. She looked from one boy to the other, and Pres could see the thoughts in her head clicking like computer keys. "I'd bet you anything that even Ben Adamson can't save the season for Tarenton," Vanessa said loudly. She was looking for a reaction and she got one. Annoyed heads immediately turned in her direction.

"Can't save the season!" Walt, who had just come out of the locker room, overheard them and dragged Olivia over. "That's crazy, Vanessa."

"Is it?" She looked around, noticing happily that she had an audience. "What do you say, Pres? Is it a bet?"

"Well, I. . . ." He hesitated just a minute.

"Pres, what are you waiting for?" Nancy stalked over, impatient with the turn of this conversation. She wanted to defend Ben, even though, clearly, he didn't need it. "You can win this bet without trying."

Pres rubbed his hand over his mouth, debating with himself. This was one time when being

37

Preston Tilford III did him no good at all. The kid with the richest father in town had the thinnest allowance. Mr. Tilford saw to it that Pres had to ask for everything, including the amount he was given a week for extras. At one point, Pres had even been reduced to taking loans from his girl friend, Kerry. Making bets that were even remotely losable would be suicide. On the other hand, it was true that there was no way he could lose this one.

"I guess you're right, Nancy," he said decisively. "How much are you in for, Vanessa? Ten bucks? Twenty?"

A group had gathered around them, watching avidly. Pres was scrappy, but Vanessa had staying power.

"That's way too low," Vanessa smirked as Ben Adamson himself walked out of the locker room. "This is the seasonal championship we're talking about, after all. How about fifty?"

Pres took a deep breath, then turned to look at Ben, who had heard the end of the conversation. "Fifty bucks says Adamson can save us," Pres agreed. "You won't let me down now, will you, Ben?"

"Me? Hey, man, the games are as good as won," Ben grinned, putting his long arms around Nancy's waist.

Vanessa smiled greedily and extended her hand. Pres shook it, noticing as he did so the deep red color of Vanessa's carefully polished nails. She was always out for blood, and this time was no exception. That didn't mean she could win the bet.

So why did he feel this terrible pain in his gut, as her long nails raked his hand? He pulled away abruptly and left the group standing there. Only Nancy turned to watch him go, but she was too happy in Ben's embrace to notice that anything was wrong with Pres.

CHAPTER

Mary Ellen ended up taking the last bus home. Patrick had been more than willing to drive her, but he had to finish putting his camera equipment away, and she was dead on her feet. There was something about a rousing game that really wiped her out. Then, too, she didn't want to give Patrick any unrealistic hopes. Driving her home once was fine, but twice in a row started to look like a pattern.

The bus let her off on Maple Lane, and she said good-night to the driver, who had the run after her father's. As she trudged up the hill toward her small turquoise house, she sighed and pulled her thin wool coat closer around her face. If only she had something nicer to come home to — a great mansion like Pres's, right on Fable Point, or a rambling ranch like Nancy's. It was just so depressing to feel on top of the world after a terrific game and then to have to come home to

. . . this *dump*. She hated herself for thinking of her own home as something to be ashamed of, but she couldn't help it. Practically everyone she knew was better off than her family.

Someday, she thought as she put her key in the door, noticing the peeling paint right around the doorbell. Someday soon, I'll be out of here, making a great living for myself in New York City. I'll have a townhouse overlooking Central Park, or maybe a stunning loft where I can see all the skyscrapers right from my bedroom window. The fantasy gave her the strength to walk inside, to see her sister, Gemma, sitting at the old formica table in the kitchen.

"Hi! How was the game? Wish I could have come, but Jennifer made me promise I'd show her how to use nail polish tonight. Was it great? Did we win?" Gemma, at thirteen, was a bundle of energy, much more mature than many kids her age. She had not been blessed with her older sister's stunning looks, but not being beautiful never seemed to bother Gemma. She was too busy enjoying life, looking into new corners, discovering new people and ideas. It was funny, but sometimes, Mary Ellen really envied her. Gemma was satisfied with her life, whereas Mary Ellen was always looking beyond to something she couldn't have.

"We creamed 'em," Mary Ellen informed her. "And the cheerleaders, needless to say, were the prod that spurred Tarenton on to victory." She went to the refrigerator and peered around inside. Fruit juice was the only thing that looked vaguely appealing right now. She poured herself

41

a tall glass, topped it with ice, and sat down beside Gemma at the table.

Her sister grinned at her. "Wouldn't have anything at all to do with that new guy, Ben, I suppose."

Mary Ellen laughed. "Well, maybe just a little."

"What do you think of my nails?" Gemma proudly displayed all ten digits, which were a party-colored assortment, from shocking pink to lime green.

"Hmm. Very punk. Don't let Mom see — she'll have a conniption." Mary Ellen gulped the last of her juice, then took the empty glass to the sink. "I'm beat. Guess I'll make this an early one. See you, Gem." She was on her way up the stairs when her sister called her back.

"Hey, wait! I almost forgot. This guy came to see you. Not a guy, actually. A *man*. An older man," she added smugly.

Mary Ellen turned around at once. "Who? Oh, come on, Gem!" she said when her sister gave her a mischievous, I'm-not-telling look.

"Yeah, he was pretty old — at least in college, I'd say. Sort of square, you know. With a suit on. And real short hair. Nice eyes, though. They were gray."

"Gemma!" Mary Ellen came over and grabbed her sister by her shoulders. "Tell me!"

"Okay, all right, keep your shirt on. What'll you give me?"

"I'll give you a smack where you'll feel it. Cough it up, kid," she said in her best private-eye voice. Every once in a while, having a little sister was a pain.

"He was from a lawyer's office in Mayville," Gemma admitted. "Said he had to see you and talk to you personally. He wouldn't say what he wanted, and Mom wasn't home from work yet, so I told him to come back. I think he said tomorrow morning."

"You *think*! Oh, Gem." Mary Ellen's mind raced furiously. What could a lawyer want with her? Well, she hadn't committed any crimes, and nobody could possibly want to sue her, except maybe Vanessa. But she didn't count because Vanessa wanted to do something awful to nearly everybody. It was all too mystifying. Could it have something to do with the cheerleaders? As captain of the squad, she'd be responsible. But they hadn't done anything that she could think of. It was all she could do to climb the creaking stairs and plunk herself down in bed.

She awoke to the sound of the doorbell ringing, and immediately her heart started pounding. Saturday mornings were for laundry, vacuuming, and all the chores she never got around to during the week. But there was something she had forgotten about this particular Saturday.

Then she remembered the lawyer who had come to see her, and she leapt out of bed. "Oh no!" she moaned, throwing on a pair of jeans and a cotton pullover, wondering, as she zipped herself up, if this was inappropriate attire for a business meeting. She brushed out the tangles in her honey-blonde hair, and stuck one of Gemma's headbands on it. There was no time for makeup. She didn't realize until she was all the way downstairs that she had forgotten her shoes and socks.

"Oh, there she is!" Mary Ellen's mother was sitting in the living room. Her visitor had his back to the staircase, but Mary Ellen could see his neat gray pinstripes from where she was. She felt like a real slob.

"Dear, this is Mr. Bransford, and he's come to see you about a certain legal matter." Mrs. Kirkwood got up and shrugged at her daughter behind Mr. Bransford's back, as if to say, You're never going to believe this! But Mary Ellen wasn't paying attention. All she could see were the awful plastic covers on the flowered chintz couch and the ugly seam in the lampshade that had come apart last week. The place was so tacky! What would this lawyer think?

"Hi!" A young man with sandy-brown hair and crinkly gray eyes extended his hand to her. He was only about her height, but he seemed taller because of his suit. He was probably in his early twenties — very early. "Call me Barry," he said before she could utter a word. He blinked a couple of times. He couldn't seem to take his eyes off her. "I know you're Mary Ellen."

"Uh, right." Boy, did that sound dumb! Don't act like such a child! she thought furiously. "I'm, ah, sorry I missed you last night, but I had a game. Basketball. I'm a cheerleader," she added.

"That's okay." Barry Bransford didn't seem interested in anything but her face. He just kept staring. "Now," he said, clearing his throat and getting down to business, "I wonder if you remember my aunt, Amanda Parsons." He began fishing around in his briefcase for something, and quickly withdrew a formal-looking document.

44

Mary Ellen frowned and looked across the room at her mother. "Uncle Roger's mother? The old recluse who came to Tommy's wedding?"

"That's it, dear. Apparently, Aunt Amanda had a stroke and died," her mother said softly. "Roger called me after the funeral. He hadn't wanted to ask us down for it, because he knew your father and I couldn't really spare the time from work for the drive to Mayville. Amanda wouldn't have cared anyway, he said. She was so strange in her later years, you see, she hardly even spoke to him." Mrs. Kirkwood shrugged and clucked her tongue disapprovingly. "Apparently lived all alone in some terrible shack on the outskirts of town. Refused to have a telephone, and she used to sit in the dark at night so she wouldn't have to turn on a light. She was *that* stingy."

Barry Bransford laughed, a little nervous chuckle. "Well, she might have been stingy, but she certainly wasn't poor. The will was read last week," he explained. "She left you an inheritance, Mary Ellen."

"She did *what*?!" Suddenly, Mary Ellen was aware of the way she was dressed and felt even worse than before. It was too embarrassing to have a man come and give her news like this, while she was standing there barefoot. She was so confused by her feelings. On the one hand, she was sorry that somebody had died. On the other, she had only met the woman once, when she was just a kid. But then there was the inheritance. She wanted to ask about it, but it seemed awful to be interested, under the circumstances.

Barry solved the problem for her by reading briskly, in a very dignified tone, from the papers before him. "And to my great-niece, Mary Ellen Kirkwood, I bequeath the sum of two thousand dollars, to be used appropriately as she deems fitting, or, should I die while she is still a minor child, as her parents deem fitting."

"Two thousand!" her mother breathed. In a family like theirs, where every penny was hard to come by, it was unthinkable to have an amount like that simply drop in their laps.

"That's. . . . Well, I'm flabbergasted," Mary Ellen stammered. For a girl who wanted money, fine clothes, and a grand life-style as badly as she did, this was a dream come true. But she felt so strange about it. Someone had died, and because of that, she had won an incredible prize. Of course she knew that good things didn't always come in the best ways, but it had never hit home as strongly before. She felt split apart about the money.

"Will you be able to come to Mayville to deal with the settlement?" He stared at her again. "My office, that is. It's standard legal procedure that you have to get the check in person. Of course, I know you're in school, so if it would be inconvenient, I guess I could get permission to bring the paperwork to you . . . if you have other obligations, I mean." He said it in such a way that she knew he wanted to see her again. And then she felt another tug at her conscience. Here was a young man, interested in her, and all because of somebody's death.

"Well, we do have reading week at school."

She looked over at her mother. "That's just before exams, Mom. We don't have any class that week. If Ardith will let me miss practice one day. . . . Mayville's only about four hours from here."

Her mother still looked dazed. "I'll speak to your father."

"Well, I'll call you," Barry said, getting up and extending his hand. "I mean, about the papers and the check," he added, his smooth face getting all flushed. "I'll ask the lawyers what can be done, and in the meantime, you can discuss it. I can't make any decision about this myself, since I'm not a lawyer — yet. Just working part-time. I'm a sophomore — pre-law at Martrain College," her told her confidentially, trying to make an impression. He succeeded.

"Well, I'm very pleased to have met you," Mary Ellen smiled at him, and she meant it. He might be square, as Gemma said, but he was ambitious, something Mary Ellen demanded in a person. Patrick was ambitious, too, of course, but for all the wrong things.

"I'll talk to you next week then," Barry said, as he got up and started out of the living room. Mary Ellen led him out to the front hall, and his eyes were still on her as he called good-bye to her mother over his shoulder.

"I'm sorry to have to bring you bad news — your aunt dying, I mean — but I hope the rest of it turns out for the best."

As she closed the door behind him, Mary Ellen understood that he wasn't just talking about the money.

CHAPTER

Nancy was trying hard to concentrate on the movie, but it was impossible. Every time she moved an arm or recrossed her legs, Ben's hand was somewhere in the vicinity. It wasn't that she didn't secretly keep hoping he'd touch her, but she felt kind of rotten about it, right in her own home. Her parents trusted her; they thought of her as pristine and well-behaved and, well, what they drippily called "a nice girl." They'd vanished into the depths of the living room, leaving Ben and Nancy alone in the basement den with the VCR and a stack of tapes. And here were Ben and Nancy, oblivious to what was playing.

"How about a soda or something?" she asked, subtly moving away from him.

"Not thirsty. Come back here," Ben said softly. He reached to pull her back, not even having to disturb his position on the couch to move his long arm.

"Not hungry, either, I guess, huh?" Nancy giggled, snuggling into the curve of his body. It felt comfortable to rest against Ben, like coming in out of a storm to a warm room with a fire raging in the fireplace. Not that he was a relaxing person to be with; there was an air of expectancy about him, and he always seemed restless, wanting more than what he had at the moment. He was as sure of himself with her as he was on the basketball court. He knew all the right moves, and he performed them effortlessly.

"How about we turn this light out, Nancy?" he asked, leaning over her head toward the lamp on the end table.

"Don't." She frowned, pulling his hand off the lamp before he could plunge them into darkness.

"Why not?" he chuckled.

"Why is that so funny, Ben?" she asked in annoyance. "Do you think so little of me that you assume I just have to do everything your way all the time?"

"Hey, sweetheart, don't get all bent about this. I only thought — "

"You don't know anything about me, and you don't want to know," she said in exasperation, more to herself than to him.

"That's not so. Maybe when we were dating before. . . . I mean, I don't deny I thought it was cool to go with a girl from the enemy camp. But I guess Romeo thought that about Juliet when they first started going together." He shrugged.

Ben threw up his hands and got up to flick off the VCR. "I really care about *you*." Then he stalked over to her. She tried not to look into his eyes, because every time she got caught in his intense gaze, she was sunk, putty in his hands. She didn't like being treated like an object, and she tried to tell herself that things hadn't changed and he was *still* treating her like an object, but it didn't work. She found herself backed up against the bookshelf, and Ben had his hands on either side of her.

"Hey, what is it, Nance? Don't you like me anymore?" he asked when she ducked under his arm.

Nancy sighed and turned her back on him. "It's not that. It's just that . . . well, I thought there was going to be more to the two of us than just . . . I don't know . . . sitting and necking and riding around in your car."

"Don't you like that?" he asked, truly puzzled.

"I do, but I like other things, too."

"Like what?" he rubbed his big hand over his chin, and he had a look on his face that clearly said, Women! Jeez!

"I like to talk about things. You know, school and sports and world events and . . . what you want to be when you grow up." She gave an embarrassed laugh, as though she wasn't sure she should mention this. Maybe she should leave well enough alone, she thought. But something inside her made her keep right on going. "I like being with other kids, too. I mean, you and I always do everything alone."

"You mean you want us to hang out with those *cheerleaders*?" He had a strange sneer on his face, which made him look more dangerous than ever.

"They're people, you know!" she exclaimed hotly. "Why do you have to categorize everyone? The cheerleaders, the basketball guys, the football jocks — honestly! You want to put everybody in tidy little boxes. Well, it doesn't work that way, Ben!"

She was really fed up now. It had seemed so good, so right to be Ben's girl — and legitimately this time. But he really wasn't the guy she wanted to believe he was. "Maybe we better say goodnight," she added hopelessly.

He stood there a minute, as if trying to decide whether it was worth it to pursue her any further. Then he smiled and reached into his back pocket. "Speaking of tidy little boxes . . ." he began. He held out a little gilt cardboard box that sat in his hand like an ant in the paw of a giant.

"For you," he added when she just stood there, staring at it.

Nancy opened the box slowly, half wondering if it was a joke and there would be some ugly rubber spider inside. She was wrong. There, lying on a snowy bed of cotton, were two lovely opal drop earrings, their irridescent beauty shimmering in the light. They had to be from Marnie's, the classiest shop in town. Nowhere else in Tarenton could he have bought anything this lovely.

Nancy was too shocked to be polite. "Why?" she asked. "I mean," she quickly went on when he looked terribly crushed, "you bought me those mittens the other day, just because I admired them and said my hands were cold. Ben, these are gorgeous, but really, I can't accept them."

"It's a present, Nance. You can't tell somebody you don't want a present." He lifted the hair beside her right ear and gently fingered the gold stud she was wearing. "How do you get this thing off, anyway? I want to see how the new ones look."

Nancy shook her head slowly, debating with herself. If she really felt uncomfortable with Ben, she shouldn't be accepting presents from him. On the other hand, maybe this was his way of telling her he really cared, that he wanted to change. And the earrings were spectacular. She sighed, then took off the ones she was wearing.

"Listen," she said softly, slipping the opals on for him to admire. "You really didn't have to do this. They're incredible, Ben, but honestly, I don't want presents from you. I just like being with you."

"They're perfect on you." He smoothed her hair back behind her ears, holding her head in his hands. Then he kissed her, slowly, sweetly, lovingly.

A voice from above brought Nancy back to earth. "Dear! Could you come up here a minute?" Her mother was calling through the closed door. Mrs. Goldstein was considerate and exceptionally tactful, remembering her own teen years. She knew enough never to barge in.

"Uh, sure, Mom. Just a sec." She moved away from Ben, reluctantly this time. "I think she's decided the date's over." Nancy grinned sheepishly.

"That's okay. Big game tomorrow — I need my beauty sleep. Good-night, babe." He kissed her again, then put an arm around her waist to escort her upstairs.

"Ben, hey, thank you," she whispered, quickly giving him a kiss on the mouth as she opened the door into the first floor hallway. "I'll wear them tomorrow night."

"You better," he said. "They're my good luck charm. I mean, *you're* my good luck charm."

"You don't need one," she told him as they walked to the door together.

That night, she fell asleep wearing the earrings, with a smile on her face. Ben was pretty wonderful, after all.

"Is everyone ready?" Mary Ellen checked her squad one last time.

"Raring to go," Pres assured her, rerolling the collar of his white turtleneck with the big crimson "T" on the front.

"Boy, there's nothing like going out and cheering for a game you know you can't lose," Walt commented, doing a couple of leg swings just to get loosened up. He and Angie were going to do a particularly strenuous series of lifts and carries during the halftime display, and he wanted to be warmed up.

Nancy checked herself one more time in the mirror. She had swept her dark hair into a ponytail, leaving little tendrils to curl around her ears. The opals were perfect with her uniform, and weren't obtrusive enough to break the no-flashy-jewelry rule Ardith had imposed for games.

"Let's go, kids!" Mary Ellen hustled them out of the practice room, and suddenly they were in the midst of the excited fans in the gym. Mary Ellen started the "Growl, Wolves, Growl" cheer and the evening was on.

Ben tipped off with the Deep River center and managed to turn and wink at Nancy as he ran down the court, ready to snatch the ball from the opposition. He let Donny make a few plays, and then he took over. An alley-oop with Andrew Polletti, then a free throw when a Deep River guard fouled against him. A hook shot, then another free throw. Ben made every basket.

"I don't know why we don't just wrap this up and go home now," Olivia grinned. She waltzed down the line of Tarenton Pompon girls, the twelve eager kids who backed up the Varsity Cheerleading Squad, and whipped them into a frenzy of excitement. She cartwheeled down their line, then did an effortless backbend and a series of handsprings.

"Gimme a *B*!"

"B!" the girls yelled back.

"Gimme an *E*!"

"E!" came the response.

"Gimme an *N*!" now yelled the whole contingent of Tarenton fans.

"N!" the girls answered.

"What dya got?"

"BEN!" everyone screamed.

At this, Ben missed a rebound, and the Deep River center was waiting to capture the ball and shoot again. Nancy could see Ben mutter to himself under his breath, but the action was going too fast for her to catch the exact curse. The ball moved back and forth between the two teams for a while, as Donny made some terrific plays, and then Deep River got the ball again. Ben lunged for the rebound and fouled against the player beside him.

"What's he doing?" Angie demanded.

"Who knows? Not so steady on his feet, is he?" Walt commented.

"He's fine. It was an accident, could have happened to anyone," Nancy growled. She felt a tight ball of discomfort right at the pit of her stomach.

"Right. Let's go in there and give them some spirit," Mary Ellen suggested, taking advantage of a time out to race onto the court and start a dazzling series of spread-eagle and straddle jumps for the "Pride" cheer.

But nothing seemed to do any good. Ben, who was a starter, was replaced by Chuck Maxwell, who didn't help one bit. Coach Cooley was jumping out of his skin, and as the score started mounting up for Deep River, he took a breath and put Ben back in the game. The two teams had been close before halftime, but after Ben fumbled again, Deep River made the score even and quickly shot ahead after that. As the opposition got stronger, the Tarenton team went to pieces. They lost the game, 60 to 55.

"I can't believe it," Pres wailed, as the cheerleaders solemnly walked through the corridor afterward. "It was in the palm of his hand. He *had* it, man. I mean, there was no way he could have missed that last rebound." He waved to the first guy out of the locker-room door. "Hey, nice try, Donny," he said.

Donny Parrish's all-American face was creased in a scowl. "Yeah, right."

"We're going out for something to eat," Angie told him, feigning a lighthearted shrug of her shoulders. "Want to come?"

"Naw. Going home to nurse my wounds, I guess," Donny said. He turned as the door to the lockers opened again and Ben walked out. "Why bother to hang around and write the obituary?"

Ben stopped right where he was, looking at the cheerleaders. Nancy stood to one side, as if trying to dissociate herself from the accusing group, but it was impossible to wipe the disappointment off her face.

"Listen, guys, I don't know what happened out there," Ben began. "I'm really sorry."

"You should be," Donny grumbled, and walked off by himself, drawing the collar of his sheepskin jacket up around his neck. He stalked the length of the corridor and left the floor, letting the big metal door slam behind him.

"Listen, I — "

"Oh, don't bother, Ben," Olivia said, putting her arm through Walt's and steering him away. "It happens to everybody once in a while."

"Sure, don't let it upset you," Pres agreed grudgingly. But when he walked off with Angie, it was clear that he was annoyed.

Mary Ellen saw Patrick coming down the hall and decided to wait for him. Even good-natured Patrick seemed a little miffed that Tarenton had lost such an easy one.

"Ben, how're ya doing?" he asked, but then didn't wait for an answer. "You want a lift, Mary Ellen?" He took her by the hand and started to lead her away. She looked back at Nancy once, then nodded. "Well, good-night, you two."

There was no response.

"I guess you're pretty ticked at me, huh?" Ben asked Nancy when they were alone in the hallway.

"Of course not. Hey, Ben, it's not all your responsibility whether Tarenton wins or loses, you know. I mean, there were nine other guys playing at one time or another tonight."

"But they counted on me. I'm the best, Nancy. I'm not saying that because I'm stuck on myself or anything. It's just a fact, that's all."

"Well, maybe you are — most of the time." She ventured a little laugh, lamely trying to ease his tense mood.

"Not funny, Nance."

"No. I know."

They stood there in the corridor together, under the harsh neon lights. Then, because neither of them had anything to say, they turned around and headed for the door.

CHAPTER 6

Tarenton won the next two games in the season easily. It was true that the Wickfield Warriors didn't have a lot of great players and the Summerville Patriots hadn't been up to par since their star center broke his leg. Still, everyone agreed that Tarenton had made a great showing at both games, and that Ben Adamson was the light at the end of the long tunnel that led to the seasonal championship. He was completely exonerated from losing the Deep River game.

But then, the next week, he was playing badly again. It was clear, even at the start of the Tarenton-Washington game that Ben wasn't going to pull them through. He seemed preoccupied, slow on his feet. Even his shooting, usually immaculate and well placed, was off. But then, Donny wasn't playing all that well, either, and the rest of the team didn't have it in them to make up so much lost ground.

"He'll pull us through in the scrimmage with Garrison on Saturday, I'm sure of it," Angie said. She and Mary Ellen were watching Pres wax his Porsche in the school parking lot. It was a beautiful afternoon, just warm enough to convince them that spring would come eventually — maybe after just a couple more blizzards. Parking lots weren't usually thought of as scenic sites, but the Tarenton lot was perched high on a hill, offering sweeping views of the lake and town beyond. Today, it was just a little hazy out, and the vista was colored with a rosy hue.

"Oh, there's no question about us winning the scrimmage," Mary Ellen nodded. "You know, I think we all made the mistake of believing that Ben Adamson was some sort of magic man, that he couldn't miss, ever. I mean, even the pros have bad games."

"Even the pros have bad seasons. That's why they get traded," Pres grumbled, scrubbing at his right fender. "This darn thing! That's just where I scraped it trying to get out from behind my father's car. How does it look?"

"For heaven's sake, Pres, if your car were any shinier it would blind mere mortals. Leave it alone!" Angie laughed.

"That's like telling him to trade it in for a garbage truck," said a sultry voice behind them.

Mary Ellen turned sharply to see Vanessa sauntering toward them. She was cuddling up close to her latest conquest, Johnny Bainbridge, the Garrison captain, and Mary Ellen felt her eyes burning as she watched the other girl approaching. She couldn't stand the way Vanessa always showed up just when you were saying something particularly innocuous, and turned it around so that it meant something you never intended it to mean. And of course, she got lots of mileage out of Patrick Henley's chosen profession. She knew how Mary Ellen felt about Patrick's garbage truck, and this gave her plenty of ammunition for her poison-tipped barbs.

"Well, Pres, that little bet we have going sure is getting exciting," Vanessa reminded him. "Want to up the ante?"

Pres's brow knitted as he swiped absentmind-his car. "Not particularly."

"Scared you'll lose, right? Worried that you'll have to pay up? Poor boy," she laughed. "But then, you could always owe it to me."

"Vannie," Pres said, his face taking on a hardness equal to hers, "I wouldn't want to owe you a dime. And I won't have to. We were just discussing the strategies that Adamson and Coach Cooley have worked out for the scrimmage. Info like this isn't supposed to get out, but I happened to have been in the locker room when they were discussing it."

She and Johnny laughed and wandered off across the parking lot to his waiting car.

The others grimaced as they watched her go. "Oh, why can't she just vanish with the winter slush?" Mary Ellen sighed. "You know, like that old, dirty gray stuff that finally melts away about the end of April."

"Vanessa's stickier than that," Angie declared. "More like old chewing gum on the bottom of a desk that you have to scrape off with a knife."

Pres had stopped working on his car and was looking off thoughtfully into the distance.

"What's the matter?" Mary Ellen prodded. She had trouble understanding how people with money could ever have problems, but today, Pres looked like he needed a friend.

"You think Adamson really could lose?" he asked, more to himself than to the girls. "It would be kinda hard for me to get fifty bucks together right now. I mean, I could do it, but I'm kinda short at the moment." He hated admitting that he had money troubles, even to his best friends on the cheerleading squad who knew him better than anyone.

"Of course he can't lose." Angie took a little wax out of the cannister and dabbed it playfully on Pres's nose. "Don't be silly."

"Even if he does," Mary Ellen said quietly, "you won't have any problem with the money, Pres. I'll lend it to you. You can give it back . . . whenever."

Pres's brow knitted as he swiped absentmindedly at his nose. "You? I mean, uh, that's a lot of dough, Melon. Too much for a loan." He would never have suggested she was poor, only that he wouldn't have expected the gesture from her.

"Look, you guys might as well know." She sat delicately on the fender, stretching her long, jean-clad legs out in front of her. "I just came into some money."

Pres crossed his arms and squinted his eyes at

her." "Oh, yeah. No, don't tell me — some old rich guy from New York offered you a modeling contract. No, wait — somebody switched your lunch bag for a sack of dollar bills."

Mary Ellen was laughing and shaking her head. "Guess again."

"Your great-great-grandmother twice removed died and left you a fortune," Angie said, getting into the spirit of it.

Mary Ellen stopped laughing. "Well, yes, sort of. It was a great-aunt I only met once. She left me two thousand dollars. Somebody named Barry Bransford — he's in college, but he's working for a lawyer's office in Mayville — he came last week to tell me about it."

"No kidding!" Pres was dumbfounded.

"Melon, that's incredible. What are you going to do with it? And what about this Barry person? Is he nice?" Angie had seen the look on her friend's face when she'd mentioned him, and knew Mary Ellen's interest wasn't completely business.

Mary Ellen tugged absently at a lock of hair that had come loose from its intricate braids. "I don't know what to do with the money," she said, avoiding the other topic. "Lend some to Pres. Put some in the bank. Maybe buy some new clothes." She smiled shyly. "And maybe convince my mom to change the slipcovers in the living room." She wasn't usually this open with her friends about how much she hated her tacky surroundings, but having the money had made her generous in spirit. And she had wanted to talk to someone about it.

But she was so wrapped up in discussing the various possibilities for her newfound wealth with Pres and Angie, that she didn't notice the shining white truck, with HENLEY TRASH emblazoned on the side, pull up on the other side of the lot. Patrick, wearing his white coveralls and a big smile, was on top of them before she knew it.

"Melon," Pres was saying, "what you should really do with all your ill-gotten gains is buy one of those new compact-disc players. They're fantastic. Have you seen them? The sound is like you're right there in the recording studio."

Patrick had sneaked up on her from behind and put his arms around her slim waist. "Hey, what's all this about Mary Ellen getting a disc player? Those things are pretty rich for her blood!"

Mary Ellen jumped when he touched her. "It's nothing, Patrick."

"Nothing! Two thousand clams is *something*, Melon!" Pres exclaimed. "Mary Ellen has been kindly remembered in some old lady's will, Patrick. She's above us all, now." He made a sweeping bow and mimed kissing the hem of her skirt. She shoved him away with one foot as she extricated herself from Patrick's arms.

"Oh, for heaven's sake!" she exclaimed in annoyance. "It's just a little money. I don't know what everyone is getting all excited about." Suddenly, she felt self-conscious. Was it because she was always looking down her nose at Patrick's garbage business and now that she had some money, she was sure they were all going to treat her like the Snooty Lady she tried hard not to be?

She felt slightly guilty, and she couldn't figure out why.

"Well, that's terrific!" Patrick was genuinely happy for her. "Isn't it terrific?" he asked the others.

"I wouldn't count on it, Pat. You know how rich girls are. They think they're better than everybody else," Pres teased.

"Pres. . . ." Mary Ellen's voice was strained, but Pres chose not to hear the threat in it.

"Yeah, that's the way it is, all right. Especially when there's some college guy involved. He sounds pretty interesting, this Larry Whats-his-face. When do we meet him, Melon?" Pres grinned.

Mary Ellen could have killed him. Why had he mentioned Barry in front of Patrick? It wasn't that Patrick was an overly jealous person, but he got so angry and depressed every time Mary Ellen decided to date someone else, even for a little while. The fact that this guy was in college gave him a definite edge. She saw Patrick's eyes narrow.

"You *don't* meet him. I'll probably never see him again, anyhow. And it's Barry, not Larry."

Patrick clearly didn't believe this for a minute. "Well, listen, you guys," he said in a cold, distant voice, "I'm a little late on my route, so I better get moving." Patrick backed away from her, already heading for his truck. He looked frustrated, not to mention ticked off.

"I'll see you later," Mary Ellen called, but he was too far away. She had hoped that he'd say something about being free right after scrimmage, and that he hoped she was, too. But he'd run off almost as though it were painful being next to her. She almost went after him, but it would have looked funny to Pres and Angie for her to have apologized for this perfectly ordinary turn of events. Anyhow, it wasn't *her* fault that Barry had come into her life bearing a barrelful of cash. What right did Patrick have to be so huffy?

"You two girls want to take a little spin in the old Porsche?" Pres asked, giving a final polish to the invisible scrape.

"Sorry, my mom made me promise I'd do the grocery shopping tonight," Angie smiled. "You two go ahead."

"I, uh, not right now, Pres." Mary Ellen rushed off quickly, not even knowing where she was racing to. All she knew was that she was on the verge of tears and felt utterly ridiculous. After all, what was that old saying? Money can't buy happiness? Well, so far, anyway, that was true. It hadn't bought her anything but Patrick's anger. And she didn't even *have* the check yet.

Everyone was ready early on Saturday. Angie was putting Olivia, Nancy, and Walt through their paces for the halftime cheers, while Pres and Mary Ellen worked on a flying fish in the corner. The sounds of the basketball team yukking it up in the lockers were audible even in the practice room next door.

"If we cream Garrison right now, there's no question we've got them in the play-off," Walt said, stopping for a slug out of the water bottle.

"This isn't a real game, though," Olivia reminded him. "It's just like another workout for the team. They always need to be playing against the clock to get any real steam up. I wouldn't worry about it, though. Ben's going to pull us through. Right, Nancy?"

"Sure."

Nancy had been quiet all week. Although nobody had commented on it, she was just not herself. Part of the time, she felt okay, not even nervous or anything. The rest of the time, though, was sheer misery. She was really getting upset about this relationship, but had no idea what she should do about it. Nancy had always thought she knew her own mind; now, though, she wondered if she even had a mind she could call her own.

Did Ben really care for her? She doubted it. If he did, then why had she found him hanging out with dumb Mindy Norris — not once, but three times? Why did he always ignore her whenever any of his basketball buddies were around? And why did he keep giving her all those presents? It was like he wanted to keep her pacified, to buy her off.

And that was the worst part of it. If she didn't like nice things — the fur mittens and the earrings, not to mention the two neat albums he'd given her last week — it would be easy. *If* she was a saint, like Angie, who could live on smiles and hugs and the thrill of being a Varsity Cheerleader; or if she was a white-hot ball of disciplined energy like Olivia, who didn't need anything but work to keep her going; or if she was the most popular girl in school and beautiful, like Mary

Ellen. But she was weak, and things meant a lot to her. Did they mean more than a serious relationship? She had to be a really shallow, superficial person if that was so.

She sighed and turned as the door to the practice room opened and Donny Parrish stuck his head in.

"Anybody seen Adamson?" Donny asked.

Nancy frowned, then shook her head. The other kids shrugged.

"Where the heck is that Adamson?" yelled Coach Cooley, who had barged in after Donny. "He knows how I am about guys who are late. This gets to me — it really does!" The coach threw up his hands and walked out of the room.

"He's never been late to a game," Pres said.

"At least, not yet." Walt made a face, then sat down dejectedly on the floor, holding the soles of his feet together. "Okay, Nancy, the ball's in your court."

"What do you mean?" she asked nervously. Everyone looked at her.

"You better call him, don't you think?" Angie suggested. "I mean, you kind of see more of him than anybody."

"What's his number?" Pres asked her. "I'll do it."

"No." Nancy was already on her way out the door. "Let me."

They all trouped down the hall after her, but stopped at the water cooler, sensing that she might want some privacy.

She took a deep breath before lifting the receiver. Then she put it down. "Somebody have a

67

dime?" she said lamely. She didn't really want to make the call, but Angie was right — the responsibility really was on her shoulders.

"Here." Pres reached into his pocket and came over to hand her the coin, then stood beside her while she dialed. They both heard the phone ring once, twice, three times.

"Hello? Ben?" Nancy said, when he answered.

"Nance! Hi!" His deep voice sounded raspy in her ear.

"Listen, what's going on? The scrimmage is about to start." She was amazed that she'd gotten him at home. What could he be thinking about?

"Hey! Is it that time already?! Oh, jeez! I . . . well . . . I was just taking a little nap, and hey — tell them I'm on my way, okay. And Nance, thanks for calling." He hung up hurriedly, and she put the receiver back down.

"What a team player," Pres grumbled. He'd heard every word.

"He'll be here," Nancy promised the waiting crew down the corridor.

"Well, he's not starting," Coach Cooley said, storming around the hallway like a wounded bear. "And don't that beat all!"

Ben was at school, in uniform, only ten minutes after the game began, and he was forced to watch Johnny Bainbridge put away basket after basket. Even Donny couldn't stop Bainbridge — the kid was a maniac, all over the court. Wherever the ball went, he was there first. Finally, after fifteen long minutes on the bench, the coach pulled Donny out and put Ben in. But it was too late. Tarenton lost the scrimmage.

Nancy had nothing to say to him afterwards. But then again, she told herself glumly as they drove away toward her house, she probably wouldn't have been awfully talkative even if their team had won. She still thought he was gorgeous, still longed to have his arms around her, and still thought she was insane ever to have agreed to date him again.

She felt miserable, and losing the game was only half of it. The other half was a more insidious, subtle feeling. Something — she wasn't sure what — was wrong, and Ben wouldn't admit it. Was it that he really didn't want to date her anymore? Vanessa had predicted that he was going to get tired of her pretty quickly. But there had to be more to it than that. In a strange way, she wished it was all her fault. But somehow, she didn't think it was.

CHAPTER

Mary Ellen was really fed up. Things seemed to be breaking down all around her, despite her best efforts to hold them together. It wasn't just losing the scrimmage, although that was pretty lousy. It wasn't just that Nancy was so preoccupied these days, she could hardly remember the difference between a handspring and a backbend. Or that Pres was so worried about losing his bet with Vanessa, he could scarcely work up the energy to lift a girl in the air during a cheer. It wasn't even Patrick's attitude ever since the topic of Barry Bransford had come up. No, it was more than that. Too much winter, maybe.

As she walked the length of the first-floor hallway, dragging her feet to postpone the inevitable — asking someone for a ride since Patrick certainly wasn't going to take her home — she wondered if having money would help any. She'd always thought her life would be perfect with just a few luxuries, and now she was going to have the opportunity to find out.

The thing was, she didn't know how she wanted the money to change her life. Did she want clothes and a fancy car? Did she want to chuck it all and leave Tarenton for good? Did she want to do the "conservative" thing and just leave the money in the bank for a rainy day?

But it's raining now, she wailed silently to herself as she walked the halls. The first thing she wanted was a vacation, and she was going to get it, no matter what. If Ardith agreed, she was going to Mayville to accept her check in person. Her parents, after some brief hesitation, had agreed that Mary Ellen should go. Mrs. Kirkwood had some time off coming to her at work, and she hadn't seen her cousin Roger in over a year, so the two of them and Gemma would set off a week from Friday in the old car.

Mary Ellen wanted to go desperately. It would be exciting, an adventure, just the boost she needed. Not that a trip from one one-horse town to another was such a big deal to most girls, but it was really something for her. Other kids' parents took them on vacations during the summer. Mary Ellen's parents stayed home and worked, and expected their kids to do the same.

Maybe the trip would shake her out of this fog of bleakness that had settled over her. She was really worried that her hunch was coming true. She was now sure that Tarenton was going to lose the seasonal championship. Ben Adamson could have won it for them, but for some reason, he wasn't shaping up to be the player everyone thought he could be. Well, romantic involvements messed a lot of people up, and he had been pretty thick with Nancy ever since he'd transferred to Tarenton. But Ben didn't seem like the type of guy to let passion come between him and a basket. It was odd.

Then there was Donny's part in all this. It was obvious, when you watched him play, that he had a huge chip on his shoulder. Mary Ellen knew Donny better than a lot of people, because she'd dated him for a while. Everyone thought Donny was always on top of things, but in reality he was just covering up for the anger brewing under the surface. She remembered all too well the night just before she broke up with him, when he'd nearly beat up Patrick out of pure jealousy. And now, he was jealous all over again, of everyone's attention being focused on Ben. Could he be messing things up and trying to make it look like it was Ben's fault? Could he be the one responsible for all the team's recent disasters?

She was still wrapped up in her somber thoughts when she felt a hand on her shoulder. She turned, startled, but she was totally astounded when she saw whose hand it was.

"Barry! What are you doing here?"

"Hey, you were wonderful out there!" He looked at her as though she'd just given an Academy-Award-winning performance. "I mean, when I was in high school, all the cheerleaders did was some rah-rah, sis-boom-bah stuff. Real dull. But this! It was like Olympic gymnastics. Really terrific!"

He smiled, and the little lines around his eyes

crinkled appealingly. Tonight he was dressed casually, in an open white shirt and a herringbone jacket with gray slacks, the kind of outfit Mary Ellen aways associated with "college guys." Of course, his hair was awfully short, and that looked kind of nerdy, but the haircut probably went with the suits he had to wear in the law office. Sort of a dress code.

But his hair didn't matter now. What mattered was how nice he was. Mary Ellen was pleased by his praise. It was the most enthusiastic any guy except Patrick had been about her in a long time. "Well, thanks. We actually weren't up to par today. You should see us when we're really going." She turned on her five-hundred watt smile, and it got the desired effect. Barry moved closer, drawn by the power she knew how to use well.

"But you still haven't told me why you're here," Mary Ellen said.

"Oh, right!" He looked embarrassed to have left out the most vital information. "Well, I went to your house to see you and your mother said you had a game tonight. Then I thought I might be able to find you before it started. But they said you were warming up, so I figured I'd wait. Glad I did."

"Well, I am, too." She smiled at him. "You drove four hours from Mayville, just to see me?"

He blushed. "Yeah, actually, I did. I like to drive. That's why I got this job, sort of. The lawyers send me out scouting around the state when they have to contact a client who's hard to find. Then, when I get to wherever I'm going, they put me up in a motel."

73

"I see." She wasn't as flattered as she had been, knowing it was all part of his job, but she was still impressed.

"Too bad about losing tonight. Tough luck for you guys."

"It sure was."

"Maybe you cheerleaders should give a few tips to the basketball players on jumping," he laughed. "Is that a sore subject?" he asked when she gave him a despairing look.

"Very." She laughed, but it had no mirth in it.

"Too bad. Well, that's the way it goes." He cleared his throat.

There was a long pause, during which time he gave her that intense stare of his. She tried to think of something bright and clever to say that would let him know in no uncertain terms that she wasn't just your average high school senior but somebody of substance.

"I was just — " she began.

"You can get your — " he said at the same time."

They both laughed nervously.

"I'm sorry," Mary Ellen went on. "You were saying?"

"Oh . . . uh . . . I just came by to tell you we can send your check through the mail. It's okay with Peters, Tankenoff, and Smiley. Those are my bosses," he added. "Things will take a little longer, because first you'll have to get the papers and sign them, and then the check will have to come to you by return mail. But if you're not really in a hurry to invest the money or use it for something, that won't make any difference."

"Oh, I see." That was strange. If she could be paid by mail, then he could have *told* her by mail, instead of driving all the way here. He'd just confirmed her belief that he was definitely interested in her, not just business.

"Actually," she told him, "I'd really like to go to Mayville. My folks have already agreed, so it's all up to my coach. I haven't asked her yet. I've been waiting for her to get in a good mood, and she hasn't been in one lately."

"Right — your coach's okay is important." He cleared his throat again. Then, in a softer voice, he said, "Ah, are you doing anything? I mean, right now? Would you like to go out for a while? You probably have to call your folks first, right?"

Mary Ellen looked at him curiously. He was so concerned with what the people in authority thought: her parents, her coach, his bosses. But that was probably part of what came with college and working and all the serious things her friends generally ignored.

"I usually go out with the squad afterwards, so it's all right if I'm late. I'd love to go out with you." She smiled again, and watched him melt right before her eyes.

"Terrific." Barry looked so pleased, she thought he was going to do a cheer right there in the hallway. They started toward to door together, and Mary Ellen felt a tingling sensation all down her back. She'd never had a date with a college guy before. Maybe things weren't so bad. Maybe life was going to whip itself into shape.

But just as Barry opened the heavy front door of Tarenton High, she saw Patrick, and her good mood disappeared like a puff of smoke in the wind. He was the last person in the world she wanted to see right now, and there he was with Donny and Andrew Poletti and Pete Raines. Well, she had no choice. She just had to plow ahead.

Lifting her head higher, she took Barry up to the assembled group. There was no point acting like she was sneaking around. After all, she told herself, this was partly business. Angie and Pres had as much as told that to Patrick earlier, so there was no reason for him to get upset.

"Hi, guys. Good work tonight, Donny," she said.

"Yeah. Not good enough, though."

Patrick was staring at her, demanding an explanation.

"Everyone, this is Barry Bransford from Mayville. He's at Martrain College." Mary Ellen tried to sound casual, as though this person were just a friend of the family or a long-lost cousin. She didn't succeed. Patrick could see what was going on between her and Barry, and he didn't like it one bit.

"Hi, nice to meet you. Good game," Barry said hesitantly. Mary Ellen was once again surprised by this guy. He actually seemed shy — in front of high school students.

The boys — everyone except Patrick — offered perfunctory hellos, but then the conversation stopped dead. Everyone was too aware of Patrick's suspicion and anger to make small talk.

Barry noticed it, too, and it made him uncomfortable. "Well, shall we get going?" he asked her.

She nodded. "See you later, guys." They walked off to Barry's car and Mary Ellen purposely didn't look back. She could feel Patrick's disappointment, and his silence hurt more than the words he didn't say.

"I'm really sorry, Mrs. Engborg, but I'd only miss one practice." Mary Ellen had waited until the very last moment, which turned out to be a mistake.

"You're repeating yourself, Mary Ellen. I'm perfectly aware of that fact. Listen, it's not me you're letting down — it's the team. I thought you kids had decided to work out by yourselves during reading week and get the new routine under your belt for the final play-offs."

"Right. We did."

"And you're the squad captain. That means your presence is vital. But if you think they can get along without you, fine. It's up to them, not me."

"You mean, you'll let me go?"

"I will. Will they? I think you should consult with the others." The coach, in her inimitable way, had given Mary Ellen enough rope with which to hang herself. That rope was made up of five other people, all with their own very firm opinions.

Why did she have to ask permission, for heaven's sake? She wasn't a child. After all, she'd just had a date with a college man, a person who was living on his own, in a dorm, working his way through school. Barry was the example to her of everything she wanted to be: independent, settled, pursuing one goal, which was his chosen career. The other evening, they'd sat together over steaming cups of coffee (not Cokes, the liquid staple of the cheerleaders), with delicate pastries (not pizza, the food most often consumed by the cheerleaders) and Mary Ellen had felt really grown up, a person in her own right. And now that she had money of her own, it put her in a different category from her friends. Pres's family was fabulously wealthy, but he had virtually nothing of his own. Nancy's parents and Walt's parents never denied their children anything, but still, it wasn't their own money. Olivia didn't care much about material possessions, and Angie just made do with what she had.

Patrick would understand where she was coming from. He'd been working as long as she could remember, even though the work he did was nothing to brag about. But the money he earned was his, and that made him closer to her new state than any of her other friends. The thing was, Patrick wasn't really interested in what she considered success. And he certainly wouldn't want to hear about her date with Barry.

Mary Ellen suddenly realized that she had taken an important step toward growing up, a step she'd been wanting to take for the longest time. It was just that temporarily, she was still being treated like a child — by her parents and her coach. She'd had to ask permission from them, and now, to top it all off, she had to ask her peers as well. It seemed totally unfair.

But she asked. She waited until the next day when they were all sitting around in the cafeteria after lunch, and then broached the subject.

"You guys wouldn't mind if I took some time off next week, would you?"

"Time off?" Olivia, to whom working out was the whole reason for her existence, couldn't imagine why anyone would want time off.

"I have to go to Mayville for a couple of days," she explained patiently. "I'd miss one practice and a couple of the extra sessions we scheduled."

"Oh great," Pres muttered. "I suppose this has something to do with that money you inherited."

"What?" Nancy woke momentarily from her daydreaming.

"You're kidding!" Walt exclaimed.

"Mary Ellen's great-aunt remembered her in her will," Angie said. "Didn't you tell them?" she asked, looking surprised. The squad always shared everthing.

"I guess I forgot." Mary Ellen looked embarrassed. Just feeling older than them had set her apart, and she'd locked them out of her good fortune by not telling them.

"Hey, that's amazing! You forgot about two thousand bucks!" Pres laughed.

"Not really. I mean, I forgot I had to make time to go get it." No use telling them that the check could be mailed to her. After all, the trip was part of the reward.

"Well, I don't know how we can spare you," Olivia grumbled. "We're short three practices as it is, and the final games are coming up."

"Not that our cheering is going to make any difference," Walt grumbled.

Nancy jumped on him immediately. "You have the worst attitude!" she growled. "With enough spirit, we can *make* our team win." She wasn't so sure of this herself now, but she had to say it. Not standing up for Ben and the team might imply that she didn't have complete faith in him. She didn't, but she didn't want the others to know.

"Well, don't take it out on me," Walt complained. "Just because you have a special interest doesn't mean you have to close your eyes every time the buzzer sounds. Losing gracefully once in a while isn't all that bad."

"Listen to Mr. Generosity," Pres quipped. "What are you, a Garrison fan now?"

"Well, if you are, you ought to disqualify yourself from the cheerleaders," Nancy told him hotly, standing up. "I wouldn't be surprised if you didn't have a little bet going like Vanessa's."

"Who, me?" Walt was instantly furious, not to mention shocked that Nancy would even suggest such a thing.

"The two of you — cut it out now!" Olivia demanded.

"I'm not doing anything! It was Nancy who — "

"Oh, for heaven's sake," Nancy spat out. "I take it back about the bet. What I meant was, you're doing a lousy job of morale-building for Tarenton. And you," she turned to Mary Ellen, "waltzing off for a trip, just when we need you the most. I have nothing to say to any of you."

Nancy stalked away from the table, as Angie

80

made a futile attempt to call her back. The five remaining cheerleaders stared at each other.

"Everything is breaking down," Mary Ellen stated, more to herself than to her friends.

"The girl has problems," Pres said, trying to make sense of this craziness that had just erupted at their table. "Listen, you might act the same if somebody you were going with was making a major disaster, instead of saving the day. Well, anyhow, what we do or don't do at three practices won't affect the outcome of the season all that much. Hey, how far is it to Mayville? Maybe a couple hundred miles, if that? If we all came with you, we could fit in some cheering *and* some studying."

"That sounds great," Angie smiled. "Not that I'd expect to get any work done at all." She frowned and rubbed her chin for a second. "I sort of promised Arne that we'd work really hard together." Then she looked at them, a mischievous grin crossing her face. "But we could work really hard at the beginning of the week, right? Then I'd be free to go."

"Then it's settled," Pres said as he got up from the table, taking his tray. "I wouldn't mind a few days away from the old folks."

"My mother's coming," Mary Ellen told him.

"Your mother is *not* my father," Pres countered. Then he stuck his hands behind his back and gave his teammates a steely stare in perfect imitation of Preston Tilford II. "I'm in favor of going. All opposed?"

"I can't go," Olivia sighed. "My mother only allows car trips for vital purposes. You know

81

how many kids are killed in car crashes every year?" she asked rhetorically. "My mother keeps track of those figures."

"Well, I'm not going if you're not," Walt said staunchly. "We agreed to spend reading week together, and I'm not giving that up." He gave her a soft kiss on the lips, which she returned. "Anyway," he added, his face breaking into a smile, "if I don't study with you, I flunk. It's as simple as that."

"I have this feeling Nancy won't go," Mary Ellen said. "Don't ask me why, but I suspect she's going to want to stick close to home next week. Close to Ben, too."

"That leaves us," Pres told Angie. "What do you say?"

"Sounds good. Let me ask at home. But that still doesn't take care of getting together to practice," Angie pointed out.

"It sort of does," Mary Ellen said, relieved to have the problem somewhat in hand. "Pres and Angie and I will work on that trio dance thing we were going to do at halftime. And Walt, Livvy, and Nancy can come up with another trio of their own to follow us. Walt, no slam-dancing with Nancy, okay? I like the idea of working three and three. No reason why the six of us have to be together all the time."

"Sounds good," Olivia nodded. "Maybe a new tactic will spur our team onto glory — *if* that's still possible. I'm kind of dreading the away game with Northfield on Saturday."

"Do you think it's just bad luck that we're losing so many?" Walt mused. "I mean, I could be talking through my hat, but I have this weird feeling that something's going on."

"You know, I've had that feeling myself lately," Olivia nodded.

"What do you mean?" Mary Ellen looked genuinely puzzled. Although she'd been concerned about Tarenton's recent losses, she'd been too wrapped up in her own situation to pay much attention to just how badly their team was doing.

"Ben was playing better a few weeks ago, wasn't he?" Angie propped her chin on her hands. "And he and Donny were working together better. I think maybe one loss is crippling to people who always expect to win. It just gets them so down, they can't perform."

"I don't think it's that." Walt shook his head. "But I'm going to find out what it really is. I have an idea." He got up, suddenly excited. The others could almost see the wheels turning in his head.

"Uh-oh. Sleuth Manners on the prowl," Pres laughed. "C'mon, you guys. Let him believe he can make a difference in the basketball season if it'll make him happy. I think I'm going to be late to class. Not that I don't want to be." He shrugged and walked off toward the door.

Mary Ellen watched the others follow him out, but she lingered at the table, playing with her napkin. Just a few more days, one more game, and she'd be free for a week. Free to do her schoolwork, patch things up with Patrick, go on a trip. She could nearly taste that freedom now. But was it sweet or bitter? That was the unknown. All she could do was wait and see.

CHAPTER

"I don't know how I could have done that!" Donny stalked up and down the Northfield locker room at halftime, a look of concern and fury on his face. "Hanging onto the rim! Jeez, if I don't know to let go when the ball is in the air by *now*, when am I going to learn?"

"Good question." Ben looked thoroughly disgusted with his teammate.

"Yeah, who are you to talk? You missed two free throws in a row, bigmouth!" Donny started toward Ben threateningly, but the coach quickly came between them.

"Listen, boys, I want everybody calm here." Coach Cooley, rivers of sweat streaming from his florid head, was trying to keep himself, as well as his players, from wanting to beat Parrish and Adamson to a pulp.

"Those two are messing it all up for us,

Coach!" Chuck Maxwell slammed a fist into one of the lockers. "Take them out!"

"All right, all right. Now, listen, Adamson. It's foul city out there. You keep racking 'em up against us. And Parrish, I coulda whaled the heck out of you for that last maneuver. What's happening?" The coach turned both guys around to face him, but he was so short, he had to stare up at them, which somewhat undermined his authoritative presence.

Pres and Walt, sitting on a bench to one side of the angry players, exchanged glances. The rest of the cheerleading squad was upstairs doing a special number for this halftime, so the two boys had decided to take a break in the locker room. Walt had on his headphones and was tapping his foot to a beat, pretending to be listening to music on his Walkman. But in reality, he was totally involved in what was going on among the team members, which was much more interesting.

"I said I was sorry," Donny shrugged. He reached for another towel and wiped his neck and chest again.

"Well, I don't have any reason to apologize," Ben said hotly. "A guy's entitled to a couple of mistakes. The captain, on the other hand," he sneered, poking a finger at Donny, "is supposed to know better than to hang onto the rim."

"Why, you — " Donny suddenly turned on him, his usually placid, all-American face twisted into a sneer. "You played just fine at the beginning of the season, Adamson, and now you're a total jerk. Why don't you call it quits and let the rest of us worry about the seasonal championship? I don't think Coach'd mind very much if you turned in your resignation right here, right now."

"Donny, that's enough." Coach Cooley took both boys aside and walked them down the line of lockers to the nearest bench, where Pres and Walt were sitting. As cheerleaders, they were generally ignored when it came to discussing team matters, and today especially, they might almost have not been there. The guys looked right through them because they didn't count.

"Now, talk to me, Big Guys." Coach Cooley was nearly begging them. "Is there something you want that I'm not giving? Better workouts? Support from your backups? A better setup?"

"I don't need my hand held, if that's what you're asking." Ben scowled. There was definitely something dangerous about him today. He was like a stick of dynamite with a very short fuse, his dark eyes darting around the lockers, the corded muscles in his neck standing out with anger. "I can do it, Coach. Just don't take me out now. I have a strategy for the next half — really, I do."

The coach gave a deep sigh, then wiped his forehead again. "It's not your strategy I'm worried about. It's all those mistakes you keep making. You know better. Ben," he said, his voice becoming firm but paternal, "you got the stuff. You can make the pros, I know it. Donny, you, too, maybe, if you try hard. But it takes discipline, it takes thought. You gotta use your head, not just your body."

"Right, Coach." Ben's tone was sarcastic, but Coach Cooley didn't pick up on it.

"Okay, everybody!" The coach left Ben and Donny sitting there and turned back to his team. "C'mon, will ya? We're all going back in there and kill 'em. We're gonna maim 'em. We'll wipe up the court with 'em. Let's do it!"

As the other basketball players slowly assembled to go back upstairs, Ben dropped his head and muttered something to himself. Then he stood up and bent from side to side, rotating his head around in a circle to work out the kinks. He walked past Pres and Walt, then waited patiently for the rest of his teammates to leave the room before striding to the open door. Donny waited for Ben to leave, then cursed and followed the others. He muttered something else as he passed Walt and Pres, but neither of them could really make it out.

"What a mess," Pres grumbled as he picked up his red and white megaphone and tapped Walt on the shoulder before starting back after the team.

Walt switched off his machine and took off his headphones. "You said a mouthful." He stowed his gear in his duffle bag and followed Pres. "And so did somebody else," he added under his breath.

The girls were perched on the sidelines, waiting for them. "You look like you swallowed a frog," Mary Ellen scolded the two boys. "One frog apiece. Let's see some smiles on those faces."

She raced back onto the floor, her arms spread wide, and started the cheer.

> "Turn around! Turn around!
> Run 'em all to the ground!
> Blow 'em out of the sky!
> Shoot 'em higher than high!
> Win it, Tarenton!
> Go, TEAM! YAAY!"

Pres and Nancy wielded their megaphones like batons, twirling them as they spun in two concentric circles. Olivia did a series of running aerial flips, propelling herself through space like a human cannonball, only to jump and push off off into Walt's waiting arms. Angie and Mary Ellen neatly balanced the outside of the circle, alternately doing straddle jumps and handsprings. The whole squad gave off energy like steam from an engine, though none of them felt the least bit enthusiastic about the outcome of this game.

"Oh, come on! Shake those pompons, girls!" Vanessa's sultry voice cut through the cheers of the crowd. She always managed to place herself in the front bleachers of any game so that she could heckle.

"Why doesn't she get laryngitis?" Olivia muttered under her breath as she stood up from a backbend.

Walt lifted her high in the air. "Why doesn't she go to another school?" was his exasperated answer.

"And she had to bring Johnny Bainbridge with her! What nerve!" Mary Ellen gave Pres a look as he hoisted her on his hip. She could tell how nervous he was getting about the bet, and Vanessa wasn't making it any easier for him.

Vanessa had never gotten over the fact that she'd been passed over by the judges when the cheering squad was selected. Her envy and greed seemed to get worse with every game she came to watch, and yet she couldn't stay away from them. It was almost as if she were punishing herself by coming to see the cheerleaders in action — which meant she had to punish all of them, simply for being good.

Which they were. Even if the basketball team was going to fail, the cheerleaders were still going to give the Tarenton crowd their money's worth. As Northfield scored again and again, Mary Ellen became more determined. She spurred the group on to new heights, partly because she was the captain and it was her job, and partly out of desperation. She had seen Patrick in the crowd, too, looking particularly glum, and her heart went out to him. It was almost as if she were trying to tell him with her frenzied cheering that everything was going to be okay between them. He didn't seem to be paying attention to her, though, no matter how hard she tried to catch his eye.

"I'm pooped." Olivia watched the clock run down as Northfield won the game, 58 to 42. "All I want is to go to sleep, which I could probably do standing up. Meet you outside the locker rooms, Walt."

Walt was silent. This wasn't his usual reaction after losing a game, Mary Ellen thought as the squad filed out of the big gym. If she didn't know him better, she'd say he was looking smug, like the cat who'd swallowed both the canary and the cream. Like he knew something and wasn't telling.

But then she saw Patrick and she completely forgot about what might be brewing in Walt's overactive imagination. There was something about the look on Patrick's face that wiped her out, made her heart feel like it weighed a thousand tons. And when he saw her, his expression changed again, and she wanted to cry.

"Patrick, please!" She turned to her squad members. "Go on without me," she directed them. "I'll get a ride."

"Better be prepared to take a bus," Pres said, assessing Patrick's glum look. But he ushered the others out of her way, leaving her alone in the corridor with the person she cared about despite her best intentions.

"Why are you treating me like this, Patrick?" she asked softly, coming over to him — not too close, but close enough.

"Like what?" he asked stonily. He wouldn't give her the satisfaction of acknowledging that anything was wrong.

"Like I suddenly don't exist," she said, exasperated.

"Oh, you mean the way you usually treat me."

His cruelty took her breath away. She shut her eyes tight, then shook her head, as if to shake off the pain. "That's so unfair. You think that if I go out for a cup of coffee with another guy it means I'm ditching you. That's just ridiculous."

"Is it? Mary Ellen, you can't deny that you're

always looking around. That it's convenient for you to have me on the back burner in case all else fails, but that basically, you'd turn on your heel and walk out of this town with the first lawyer who asked you. Or doctor. Or movie director, or head of some modeling agency. You're on the lookout for the opportunities, and I've just woken up to the fact that I will never be one of them. It's the sad truth," he added when she opened her mouth to protest.

"You make it sound like I have no feelings about you at all," Mary Ellen said weakly. "And I do."

"Feelings are great up to a point, Mary Ellen. But I'm the kind of guy for whom actions speak a lot louder."

She sighed, wondering how best to explain this to him. She thought about being emotional but, at the last second, opted for practicality. "That person you saw me with is working for the law office who's handling my great-aunt's estate."

"So why can't you see him in the law office like a client? Why do you go out with him after a a game?"

"Patrick, you twist everything around! I really — "

"No, really. I want an answer. And I'm not budging till you give me one. What's he got that I haven't got?"

He put his hands on his hips and glowered down at her, daring her to even suggest that he was lacking in any way. She couldn't answer him, because it occurred to her that if she started comparing, Barry Bransford might very well end up a poor second. Patrick was gorgeous, he was sexy, he was kind — he was everything a girl could ever want in a guy, except for the one glaring fact: He didn't want to get out of Tarenton. And she did.

"Well," she began huffily, as if she was annoyed that he didn't know, "he's in college, he's mature, he has a responsible job, and he's going places."

"And he wears a three-piece suit in the office, right? Well, lady, I can wear three-piece suits with the best of them. *And* drive a garbage truck, too." With that, he swept her into his arms and embraced her with a kind of anguish and desperation that firmly stated his position. His kiss was insistent, his mouth molding hers and speaking to her in a mesmerizing, marvelous language. When he finally let her go, minutes later, she was breathless.

"So don't see him again," Patrick told her, the hint of a smile creeping into his dark, deep eyes. He liked the fact that he could shake Mary Ellen's mind with a touch.

She got hold of herself just in time. "I won't promise you that."

"I won't sit around forever, Mary Ellen. Believe me, I won't. The other day, when I saw you with that guy, I thought, Hey, what am I kicking myself around the block about? Am I some kind of masochist who keeps coming back for more?" He shook his head sadly, but there was a firmness about him, a dedication to the principles that guided him and made him the wonderful person he was.

"Patrick. . . ." Mary Ellen was so confused, she didn't know where to begin. Basically, she knew he was right, and there was no defense she could offer on her own behalf. But on the other hand, she hated being told that she was an utterly callous person, one who made friends and discarded them like so much Christmas wrapping.

"I'm not an idiot, see, and I really hate being treated like one. Even by you." He took a step away from her, then continued. "I will always want you. I can't imagine ever forgetting you. But I'll be damned if I'm going to let you tear me up in little pieces and throw me away. Think about it, Mary Ellen."

He turned and walked away, his solid presence a tantalizing and frustrating reminder that he was the only person she'd ever known who could make her melt into a delicious puddle of longing, just by looking at her. And he was still the best friend she'd ever had — most of the time. Was she about to kill all that? And what would it gain her? A few dates with a sort of dull guy who happened to be a little older and happened to have a prestigious job.

But she couldn't dwell on this right here or right now. If she didn't get moving, she would be stuck in Northfield overnight. She ran to the front door of the school and was barely able to flag down one of the last Tarenton cars in the parking lot, the station wagon that belonged to the Eismar twins' mother. But as she climbed inside and settled back for the ride, she wondered what she was doing — with her life, with her friendships, with her very soul.

* * *

"Now just sit there a second and listen to this."
Walt pushed the rewind button on his tape recorder and Olivia looked at him expectantly.
Then he pushed PLAY and the tape proceeded to
turn.

"We're gonna maim 'em. We'll wipe up the
courts with 'em. Let's do it!" Coach Cooley's less
than pearly tones emanated from the machine.

"I can't believe this! You *taped* the guys in the
locker room at halftime!" Olivia looked puzzled.
She sat back in the Jeep and stared at her boyfriend in the dark. "What is this? Watergate?"

"Keep listening," Walt counseled her.

There was a lot of background noise and the
sound of benches being scraped. A couple of
curses. Then, a muttered phrase she couldn't quite
make out. Then, the sound of a lot of guys making
general noise. Finally, another phrase that
sounded like, "Can't make it."

"Well, what does that prove?" Olivia sat back
and crossed her arms.

"Didn't you hear him say that? He as much as
admitted it."

Olivia rolled her eyes. "I have absolutely not a
clue as to what you're talking about."

"Donny — Donny Parrish. I taped him saying,
'I can't keep this up any more. I can't make it.'
Didn't you hear that?" Walt couldn't believe that
this wonderful, talented, exceptionally brilliant
girl could be so dense. "I got him dead to rights.
And you told me this tape recorder was a stupid
purchase. Ha!"

"Oh, Walt." Olivia ran the tape back, then

94

played it again. She shook her head, then repeated the process twice more. "I only hear, 'Can't make it.' He could have meant he couldn't make another basket, for heaven's sake. This doesn't prove a thing."

"But if you'd been there, Livvy! The expression on his face — I just know he was saying he was throwing the games. I know it!"

"Expressions do not translate into proof, dummy, especially not on a tape recorder. All you have here are three little words and a lot of benches scraping and guys talking. Nothing more. And anyhow, why would Donny *want* Tarenton to lose?"

Walt sighed, then reached over to bop his girl friend on the head. "Don't you see? He's been the star at Tarenton for three whole years now — nearly won the championship for us last year single-handed. And he would have, too, if it hadn't been for Ben. Do you know what that means to a basketball hero? To suddenly be replaced as first-string player by his arch enemy. Captain or not, he still has to take a backseat to Ben. So naturally, he wants Ben to look as bad as possible. He wants that so much, he's willing to let us lose the championship." He sat back, a smug look on his face. He was enormously pleased to have deduced this so logically. "For Donny to let Ben win the championship for Tarenton now is . . . I don't know, like expecting Pres to trade in his Porsche for a Dodge. Or Mary Ellen to go a day without washing her hair. It's unnatural."

"Okay, Mr. Brains. So why was he killing himself to win some of the games? You can see he's

95

doing his best — or was, until a couple of weeks ago."

"Because that's the whole point. Because it's an act. I'm sure of it." Walt's earnest face was flushed with his terrible discovery.

"I'm still not buying it," Olivia said. Then she sidled over to him on the seat and ran her delicate fingers across his face. "Such a fevered brow." She leaned close and kissed it, then gently kissed his lips. "I think you should let this rest, Walt. A little smirk on the guy's face and a couple of incriminating words is not going to stand up in any court of law. Face it, if Donny does want us to lose the championship — and I'm still not convinced that he does — your tape won't change a thing."

Walt looked very pensive, then shrugged. He turned the key in the ignition and the Jeep sprang to life. But Walt wasn't going anywhere just yet. "I know what I saw — and what I heard. And I have the perfect opportunity to get close to him Saturday at the Garrison game. So I'm going to do it again."

"Yeah, well, you better pray that he's a blabbermouth the next time you tape him."

They rode in silence for a while, both of them depressed about the current state of affairs. You could only do so much as a cheerleader, and after that, you had to sit back on the sidelines and let the team finish the job. But this time, Walt seemed to feel that the responsibility for victory was all his. That burden felt awfully heavy, and it didn't make him happy.

"Hey," Olivia said when they'd gone several

miles in silence. "Is it legal to tape another person without their knowing?"

"No, I don't think it is."

"Then you better quit while you're ahead," she said in a worried voice.

"No problem. I'll tell him exactly what I'm doing." Walt had a very silly grin on his face.

"You'll what?" Olivia was incredulous.

"Listen, would you believe it if I told you I was taping you?"

Olivia considered this a moment. "No. No, I'd think you were putting me on."

"Precisely." He put his foot down on the accelerator and they took off, heading for Walt's house deep in the woods. He drove with exceptional concentration, seemingly deeply interested on the road in front of him. In reality, however, he was busy concocting newer and more devious plans for espionage. Sleuth Manners was going to get to the bottom of this . . . or know the reason why.

CHAPTER

"You're disappointed in me — say it." Ben sat in front of Nancy on the floor of her living room and she sat over by the window, watching the light snow falling on the front yard. It was very hard for her to look Ben in the eye tonight. "Well, don't be," he continued. "The war isn't over till the last battle's won." He was surprisingly sure of himself, almost cocky, and there was nothing hang-dog about the expression on his face.

"I know. I didn't say anything."

"But you thought it. I can read your thoughts — I know you pretty well by now, sweetheart." He got up and came over to her, taking her gently by the nape of her neck to turn her around to face him. He was smiling when he leaned down to claim a kiss — a kiss she would have bestowed gladly, she realized, if only he'd won.

Why? she wondered, pulling away, shocked at what she'd just thought. What difference should that make in our relationship? I want to like him, but something about him makes me uncomfortable. Is it me, or is it just that we're not made for each other? But she had to admit that it was easier to like a hero than a failure, and she was beginning to think that even if he wasn't exactly failing, Ben certainly was letting everybody down.

"Talk to me, sweetheart. Get it out in the open," Ben said when he felt her reluctance to stay close to him.

Nancy took a deep breath, then said, "Maybe we shouldn't see each other for a while."

He scowled at her. "What, because I'm not such a big cheese anymore? Suddenly you don't want to be seen with me? Look, I'm not the kind of guy to point fingers, but I'm not the one responsible for all this. And you and everybody else knows who is. Donny Parrish just can't take competition, especially not from inside. But if you want to blame me. . . ." He shrugged, implying that she was making a big mistake.

"Don't be ridiculous. That has nothing to do with it. It's just . . . well, maybe your concentration is a little scattered these days. And what with the big Garrison game coming up right after reading week, maybe it would be a good idea to cool it — till then. Afterwards, we could talk, see how we both felt."

"I know how I feel." He put one huge hand around her waist, then with the other, reached up to touch the delicate opal earring that he had given her. It was a reminder to both of them that, since she had accepted his presents, she had accepted him. Until now.

"Ben, the guys on the team are really up in arms. I mean, they're having a hard time understanding what's wrong. I know every athlete has lapses, but — "

"That's right, sweetie. And Donny's had more than his share in the past month. I guess when I see him floundering around that court, it brings me down, too." He surprised her by bursting into laughter. "You just wait. I'm going to pull it out of reverse into overdrive. Honest. I'll show those Garrison bozos."

"How do you know? How come you're so sure?" she asked.

"Because I am, that's why. Come on back, sweets. Don't be so low. There's nothing to worry about."

Nancy said nothing. She knew there was a great deal to worry about, because if Tarenton did *not* beat Garrison next Saturday, they wouldn't make the play-offs. And there would go the championship, right back into enemy territory. And there was something else. Why did Ben seem so confident that he could win the next game, when he'd performed so poorly in the last three? Could it possibly be that he was —

No! The idea was so repellent to Nancy that she cancelled it from her mind as soon as she'd thought of it. It wasn't possible that he was doing this on purpose — to make Donny look bad. He couldn't be losing a few, then winning the crucial ones. He couldn't be toying with the Tarenton games like a cat playing with a mouse. *Could he?*

She was certain that he wasn't that kind of manipulator. People might say a lot of bad things about Ben — that he was egocentric, insensitive, that he had the looks and attitude of a real tough guy — but no one would ever call him a liar or a cheat. And as for purposely messing up another kid's reputation, he simply wasn't capable of that.

"So what are we doing next Saturday night?" Ben asked, quickly changing the subject. "How about a late dinner at Charlie's out in Cedar Point?" He grinned, waiting for her reaction.

"Charlie's! But that's the most expensive restaurant in town. I went there with my folks on my birthday."

"Well. . . ." Ben's grin got considerably wider. "Did you like it?"

"Yes, sure, it was great. But Ben, that's too much money."

"Not for you, Nance. It'll be our celebration. Our victory dinner in advance. To commemorate the fact that Tarenton is going to beat every other basketball team in the league — starting with Garrison. Okay," he said, grabbing his letter jacket off the back of the couch and starting for the door. "It's a date for after the game. Dress up real pretty, okay?" he teased her, planting a firm kiss on her lips.

Nancy closed the door behind him and watched him climb behind the wheel of his Isuzu. The smile on her face was strained, but Ben couldn't see that in the dark. The doubt that had been eating at her for the past weeks had blossomed into full-blown suspicion, and he had just confirmed her worst fears. If she didn't act on them at once, Tarenton was going to be in real trouble.

Olivia was relieved that it was finally reading week and she could knuckle down to business. She wouldn't have said she was bored with school, exactly, but some of her classes were so excruciatingly dull, she wanted to scream. She liked things done efficiently and expertly, whether it was executing a perfect triple back flip or memorizing every important date in the Civil War. She was just that kind of person.

The only problem was getting the right atmosphere for studying, because the Evans' house was never really quiet. Every time things settled down and she and Walt were enjoying the peace and silence, her mother would pop her head in and ask if they needed anything, if they had enough light, if they wanted some other chairs with straighter backs, if their pencils needed sharpening. And of course, how much longer Walt would be staying. It was enough to drive a sane person totally and absolutely batty.

"We're fine, Mother," Olivia said for the first hour every time her mother barged in on them. "We need some concentrated time with no interruptions," she said pointedly the next time the door opened. But when it happened for the fifth time, there was no stopping Olivia.

"For heaven's sake, Mother! This is reading week! We are reading — an activity that demands an attention span longer than three minutes in duration! If you'd just leave us alone and

102

go away, we'd be perfectly all right!" she blurted out, scarcely aware of Walt's restraining hand on her shoulder.

"Well, if that's the way you feel — " Mrs. Evans rushed out in a huff. "I certainly won't bother you again."

"Yes, you will," Olivia muttered to the closing door. "Oh, come on, Walt. Let's get out of here and go to your house. At least your parents have something better to do with their time than check to see if we're breathing." Without waiting for his response, she clomped down the stairs and into the front hallway, marching past her mother into the den, where her father sat rivetted to the television set.

"Walt and I will be at his house," Olivia enunciated carefully, as though she were trying to communicate with someone who didn't speak English. She did not ask permission, realizing if she did so, her father would only pass off the request to her mother, the way he always did. And then they'd be back to square one.

The Manners' house wasn't much quieter than Olivia's, but at least the turmoil was self-contained and didn't bother Walt and Livvy. That was because when Walt's parents were home, they were working. People with tight deadlines don't have the time *or* the inclination to nag their children about the least little thing. Mr. and Mrs. Manners were either taping their segments for the next morning's TV show or editing scripts or having story conferences. The nice thing, as Olivia had noticed immediately the first time she was there, was that the Manners never made her feel like a kid. They seemed to respect her and even occasionally asked her opinions on various subjects. Walt used to grit his teeth whenever they did this.

"Why don't they ever ask me what *I* think?" he'd grumbled to Olivia.

"Because you're their son. Everybody's parents think their kids are dodos. Look at mine."

"But I'm clever, witty, talented, and informed," he protested.

"You're still their son." Olivia had grinned.

Today, Mr. and Mrs. Manners looked like they were up to their ears in work, so the kids tiptoed around them, nodding on their way into the kitchen. Walt had just demolished one plate of cookies over at Livvy's house, but he was desperately in need of another. He couldn't seem to study without a plate of something in front of him.

"It's really getting out of control," they heard Mrs. Manners saying through the half-open door. "Corruption in the high schools is rife. I don't think two TV shows on the subject will scrape the surface of the problem. We should do a whole week on it. What do you think?"

Her husband nodded his emphatic agreement. "Absolutely. I mean, it's everywhere you look. The drugs, the dropping out, the crime, the cheating. . . . My only concern is that it's going to be too much of a downer for our audience."

The animated living room conversation kept drifting back to Walt and Livvy. Clearly, this was a subject on which they should be consulted.

They were the experts, after all. Olivia chimed in first.

"Corruption in squeaky clean Tarenton High?! You've got to be kidding." She got up and walked into the living room. "C'mon, folks. We don't have any crime in this town. Walt told me that's why you decided to live here. And if there's anyone concerned about a safe environment for her kid, it's my mother. She wouldn't stay here a second if she believed there were" — she turned back to Walt, who was standing in the doorway — "evil influences in our schools."

"I think you've closed your eyes to the truth, Olivia," Mr. Manners said rather grimly. "Just think about it a minute."

"Yeah, Livvy," Walt agreed. "I keep telling you — there's lots of bad stuff going on. It's funny you should bring this up now, Dad, because just a few nights ago in the locker room during halftime, I taped a — "

Olivia cut him off at once. "When you were taping up your *ankle* downstairs, I was busy out there cheering," she said with forced animation. "And I saw all those potential criminals jumping around and having a great time playing basketball." She came around in back of him and gave him a swift jab in the heel, letting him know, in no uncertain terms, that the topic of taping was closed.

"Yeah, well, I still think Dad and Mom have a point," Walt said glumly. "You're just too innocent to see what goes on in front of your nose, Livvy."

105

"All right, dear," Mrs. Manners said, turning back to her husband. "Let's start with drugs, shall we? That's the one the parents are most terrified and least informed about. I have this huge file of material. . . ."

Walt and Olivia wandered back into the kitchen, leaving the Manners to their work. They both opened their books, and Walt put a cookie in his mouth, chewing solemnly as he sat staring into space. "I know you don't want me to talk about it, Livvy, but now it's going to be on TV, so you and a lot of other people are going to find out the truth."

Olivia made a face at him. "Not so loud, buddy. Any more cracks about your illegal taping and you're going to be the subject of your own parents' expose," she whispered pointedly. "So let's not cast any stones at Donny Parrish, shall we?"

He shrugged and reached for another cookie. "Just wait," he said calmly. "Next Saturday, you'll see I'm right. And so will everybody else."

Mary Ellen decided to pack everything she could possibly imagine she might want to wear in Mayville, even if she only put on half of what she brought.

"I don't see why you're taking all that stuff," Gemma scoffed as she sat on the bed opposite her sister's in the tiny room they shared. "It's not like you're going to New York or Paris or anything. Just to Uncle Roger's."

"You wouldn't understand, Gemma," Mary

Ellen said, a bit patronizingly. "You never know what might come up. I have to be prepared, just in case." She had one good white silk blouse, so naturally, that came out of the closet first. Her plain blue A-line skirt for her meeting with the lawyers, with a red belt and scarf for accents. Then a few pairs of jeans, some corduroy pants, three turtlenecks, and a couple of plaid, button-down shirts. She was just trying to figure out whether she should take her stunning, but uncomfortable, high-heeled boots when the phone rang.

Gemma sprinted to the hallway to get it and was back two seconds later, panting and grinning, to announce that "gorgeous Pres Tilford" was on the phone.

Mary Ellen bopped her lovingly on the head. "I promise you can sit next to him in the car tomorrow. I'll arrange it," she said magnanimously.

"Honest? Can I? What'll I say to him? He'll think I'm such a little dope!" Gemma was beside herself.

"He'll think you're a little dope whose sister beat her up if you don't keep quiet — *now!*" Mary Ellen said with her hand over the receiver.

"Oh, sorry. I'll get lost," Gemma said, slapping a hand over her mouth and running down the stairs.

"Hi, Pres," Mary Ellen said into the phone after her sister had disappeared.

"Just wanted to let you know that Angie's brother Al is bringing us both over about eight tomorrow A.M. My folks can't believe their good luck — getting me out of their hair for a whole three days. Wow!"

Mary Ellen laughed appreciatively. "Don't bring a lot of luggage. Between everything my mom wants to cart along to my uncle's house, and the accumulated garbage of Gemma, Angie, and me, there's hardly going to be room for you and a toothbrush."

"No problem," he said. "I travel light. Did you get hold of Nancy?"

"Yeah. She sounded pretty weird, kind of like she wasn't listening to much of what I was saying, but she did promise to make a date with Walt and Olivia over the next couple of days so they can work out. I guess we can trust Livvy to whip the other two into shape while we're away. I wish there was something we could do for Nancy, though. She's never been this riled up over a guy before."

"Yes, she was. I remember it distinctly — the last time she went out with Ben," Pres reminded her. "Well, maybe after we've lost the game on Saturday, she'll think again about dating him."

"Pres! Don't say that," Mary Ellen scolded. "Don't you even *think* it."

"Look," Pres said mournfully, "I'm the one who's going to suffer most if we don't win. That bet I made with Vanessa looms larger every day."

Mary Ellen shook her head in annoyance at the mere mention of Vanessa. "It was only a handshake bet."

"I wouldn't shake her hand!" Pres growled. "Handshakes imply friendship, and my feelings about that girl are far from friendly these days."

"Look, Pres," Mary Ellen chose her words carefully, "I'm going to get my check from Barry's lawyers tomorrow. As soon as we're back in Tarenton, I'll deposit it, and when it's cleared, the fifty dollars is yours. I mean that."

"I know you do. Thanks, Melon."

She could feel the warmth of his smile over the phone wires. "So, I'll see you in the morning. Coffee will be served at eight, promptly," she giggled.

"Good-night. Sleep tight," he signed off.

As soon as she hung up, the phone rang again. It was Angie, calling to ask a few last-minute wardrobe questions. The girls compared their packing lists, and then moved onto the topic of how much studying and practicing they might get done in Mayville. "Gemma and Mom and I will have to spend some time with Uncle Roger, of course," Mary Ellen said. "But you and Pres can do whatever you like then. Maybe the mornings would be good for rehearsal — how about it?"

"Fine with me. I guess you'll want one evening to yourself anyway." Angie tried not to sound slightly envious.

"For what?"

"A date with Barry, you idiot. Anyhow, whatever happens, it'll be different, which means it'll be fun. See you, Mary Ellen."

"Good-night." As Mary Ellen put down the receiver, she realized that she hadn't thought much about Barry Bransford since the evening they'd had coffee together. It was strange. He was just the kind of guy she should be crazy about. And yet, something was missing. When she imagined his face before her, violins did not start to play, nor did trumpets peal. As much as she might have wanted to, she just couldn't work up any excitement about him. It was odd, that although Barry personified everything she thought a boyfriend ought to be — rich, attractive, sophisticated — he never caused any passion to erupt inside her. The way Patrick did, for example.

She was mulling over this dilemma when she heard music outside. Someone's car radio? No, it was live music — a badly strummed guitar. As she peered out the hall window, she could make out a figure, all dressed in white, standing down in the driveway. She blinked, and looked again. It was Patrick, wearing his white coveralls. His face, wearing a rather bemused smile, was tilted up toward her. In his deep, rumbling baritone, he sang a simple tune he'd clearly just made up.

> "Oh, sweet lady, hear my plea,
> I'm the one for you.
> Clothes don't make the man, you see,
> Tell me that's not true.
>
> "I'm no lawyer, I'm no prince,
> I'm no shining knight.
> But this heart that loves you so,
> Will see you through the night."

As the last chord died away, he put his guitar down on the pavement and unzipped the coveralls. Stepping into the spill from the porch light, he thrust out both arms and did a leisurely spin

110

around so that she could appreciate his outfit. He was wearing a blue, pinstriped, three-piece suit and a starched white shirt with a burgundy tie. Mary Ellen had to laugh at the strange picture he presented.

"This is it, kid. Your own homegrown boy spiffed up with a little spit and polish," he called up to her.

"You look lovely," she told him, meaning it. She was about to tell him to stay where he was, that she'd come down, when he stopped her right in her tracks with a pointed question.

"So which is the real person, Mary Ellen?" he asked philosophically, holding up the garbage-man's coveralls beside his emaculate business clothes. "Or are they one and the same? And does it make any real difference to you? Think about that when you're in Mayville, will you?"

He picked up the guitar and, humming the tune slowly and deliberately, he strolled down the driveway toward his truck. As he drove away, Mary Ellen could see the words HENLEY TRASH for at least half a block before he turned the corner.

She stood with her elbows propped on the windowsill, looking down thoughtfully at the spot where Patrick had just serenaded her. Had he intended to make her feel rotten, or did he just want to call her up short on her dumb values? She was vain and pompous, more concerned with the suit than the person wearing it. But Mary Ellen had been forced to come to a realization tonight. She had to stop judging life on its appearances, and she had to do it very soon. If she didn't, Patrick would vanish from her life. What was the old fairy tale about the vain and pompous emperor? His exquisite new clothes had turned out to be nothing but thin air, after all.

Mary Ellen shut the window and returned to her room to finish packing. Much to her sister's amazement, she emptied her stuffed suitcase and started over. This time, she packed only what she needed.

CHAPTER

Mayville was a really pretty town with wide streets and mammoth Victorian houses, complete with gingerbread trim and spacious, columned porches. There were windowed turrets reaching to the sky, which today was a pearly blue with fluffy clouds flying overhead — a perfect, picture-book winter sky.

The ride down had been a quiet one, with everyone immersed in his or her own thoughts. Mary Ellen was still preoccupied with Patrick, and the fact that she wished she'd had a chance to talk to him before she left. She realized that she would really rather be spending tonight with him than with Barry Bransford. She just hoped it wasn't too late to tell Patrick that.

Angie was worried about Saturday's game. Although she knew the squad didn't need all that much additional rehearsal, she didn't like the idea of them being separated for three whole days.

Especially with Nancy in the mood that she was in. Arne had been in a mood when she left, too. It was impossible to explain to someone for whom schoolwork was the whole crux of existence, why she needed a break. She liked Arne, she admired him enormously, but they just didn't have a meeting of the minds about a lot of things.

Pres was thinking about the game, too, but he was more concerned about his bet with Vanessa than anything else. Even if Mary Ellen lent him the money, he'd have to pay her back, and he couldn't see how the was going to do that except by getting a job. One thing he had to be honest about — he liked playing better than working, which meant that anything he did in order to earn money was going to be a real downer. Still, he was going to have to buckle down and do it.

As the Kirkwood station wagon made its way into the center of town, weaving through the light traffic, Angie read the directions to Uncle Roger's house aloud. Gemma, sitting beside Pres, was sleeping quietly, her head on his shoulder, and Mary Ellen started scanning the streets eagerly, imagining what life in a college town might be like.

"This is a lot more attractive than our part of Tarenton," Mrs. Kirkwood noted.

Angie protested. "I think our lake is absolutely gorgeous, not to mention all the woods right on the outskirts of town. I can't see living anywhere else."

Mary Ellen listened quietly, but she never would have agreed with Angie. Even Mayville, by no means a major metropolis, made her feel a tingling of excitement. The idea of a city built around a college was fascinating to her. There would be people here who discussed Important Subjects at breakfast, who casually referred to current events and great literature and astrophysics. Mary Ellen was not an intellectual, but she craved the kind of life that inspired her onto bigger things, more important ideas. She had outgrown her hometown; she was sure that it was time for her to move on. On the other hand, she hadn't outgrown Patrick, and Tarenton was where he meant to stay.

"Oh, look! It's Peters, Tankenoff, and Smiley. Isn't that where we're going this afternoon?" Angie turned to ask Mary Ellen. "Nice offices."

They drove on for a few more blocks, then took a left and found themselves right in the midst of a beautiful residential area. The houses were all different — some Victorian, some colonial, some ranch, but somehow they all seemed to fit together nicely in a loose, hodgepodge of architectural styles.

"Where are we?" Gemma yawned and stretched, then noticed her arm resting on top of Pres's. She picked it up as though she'd burned it. "I'm really sorry, Pres! Really!"

"Hey, no problem," he grinned, pleased that he even had an intoxicating effect on younger women. "We're here. It's your uncle's house. Right, Melon?"

Uncle Roger, a widower, lived by himself in a small ranch house surrounded by towering maples. He was a retired Navy man who, according to Mrs. Kirkwood, had moved here despite his own desire to always be close to some large body of water, because Mayville was where his wife wanted to be. Even now, when he was on his own and could have gone anywhere in the world, he claimed it was too late in life for him to pull up stakes and move. Still, he longed for the sea and talked about it constantly.

Mary Ellen, Pres, Angie, and Gemma sat in the big kitchen with the adults, making chitchat and drinking Cokes for a couple of hours, talking about school and Tarenton and the problems they were having with their basketball season. Uncle Roger seemed a bit confused when they told him that Pres was a cheerleader, too, but he wasn't the kind of man to question what anyone else did for fun. After an hour or so, Mrs. Kirkwood claimed she needed a nap, and Mary Ellen realized that this was their cue to get out of the house.

"I have that appointment with the lawyer, Uncle Roger, and Pres and Angie said they'd come, too," she explained. "I guess we'll be back late, because my friend Barry said he'd show us around the Martrain campus. But we'll be here for dinner if you want us," she said hastily when her mother gave her a look.

"Well, you know, kids," Uncle Roger said, "if you could amuse yourselves for a while tonight, it might be nice. I promised I'd take your mother out on the town the last time she and your dad were here five years ago, and I never did. So I owe her one."

Pres looked noticeably happier. He was never that thrilled about being around adults when he didn't have to be. "We'll grab something to eat at the college cafeteria, then. See you guys later." He got up and took the car keys that were lying on the kitchen table.

"Sure you don't want me to drive you?" Uncle Roger asked.

"No, that's okay. Angie's become a terrific map-reader. We'll make it all right."

"Have a good time," Gemma sighed. She was still too young to pal around with her sister's friends, and she knew what her mother would say if she begged to go with them. She knew what Mary Ellen would say, too.

Mary Ellen and Angie changed their clothes and raced downstiars. Pres was waiting impatiently for them beside the car.

"Let's go, girls. I want to get the formalities over so we can get on over to the Martrain campus." He grinned.

"And I thought you were bound for Princeton," Mary Ellen teased him. "I wouldn't think a podunk little place like Martrain would be that fascinating to you."

"Princeton is where my *dad* wants me to go. *I'm* not sure," Pres said. "Anyhow, college is college, right? And that means parties, wine, women, and song, with no parents hanging around."

"Oh, that's all you ever think about," Angie declared as Pres pulled into the open space in front of the lawyer's office. "You don't even remember why we're here. Have a little respect for Mary Ellen's great-aunt, would you?"

"Sorry," Pres sighed, turning off the engine and turning to the two girls. "It's not exactly a totally fun occasion, I know that."

"Well, don't get all maudlin about it," Mary Ellen assured him. "I didn't know her at all. I still can't believe she left me all that money." She opened the door and stepped out into the sunny afternoon.

"You know, you haven't told us what you're going to do with it," Angie reminded her.

"I really don't know," Mary Ellen shrugged. "Aside from Vanessa's bet — if we have to pay her off, which I don't think we will because Tarenton just *has* to win on Saturday — " she took a breath " — well, I could do anything. Get an apartment in New York, buy a whole new wardrobe, go to Europe, go to college. Who knows!" She went up to the door of the office and rang the bell.

"Whoa! Wait a second." Pres put a hand on her shoulder. "I don't know where you've been getting your info lately, but those things you just mentioned cost a lot more than two thousand bucks. I know how much you want bright lights and action, Melon, but don't get carried away just because you have this little nest egg. Yeah, you could manage a quick trip to Europe, maybe, if you watched every penny. But that'd about wipe you out. College, sure, the money could pay for a few courses at a state school. As for a place in New York City, well, these days you couldn't rent a piece of a subway car for that little money."

Mary Ellen frowned, caught up short by her economic ignorance. "Hmm. I didn't realize —" she began, but then the door opened and Barry was standing in front of her, grinning expectantly. When he saw the other two, the elation in his face dimmed a bit, but he was still thrilled to see Mary Ellen.

"Hi, Barry." She noticed his three-piece suit immediately. He didn't look anywhere near as good in it as Patrick had in his. "This is Pres Tilford and Angie Poletti. You probably remember them cheering at the game. They came along to keep me company."

Barry's vague hello confirmed Mary Ellen's opinion that he hadn't seen anyone but her at that game. She was beginning to feel just a little trapped, like she'd given him reason to believe that she was really interested when she wasn't.

"Well, come in, all of you. You just have to sign a few papers, Mary Ellen, and then you can have your check. I, ah, I hoped you'd be free for dinner tonight," he said in a quieter voice.

She smiled at him, but this time she made sure to tone down the wattage of her glow. "We'd all really love to see the campus, if that's okay with you. And then we're available for the evening. My mom and uncle are letting us off scot free," she joked.

Angie watched her friend carefully, understanding completely what was going on. Mary Ellen had wanted company on this trip for a reason, and it wasn't just so the squad could practice together. She wanted protection from a relationship that she felt uncomfortable with. As Angie sat in the reception area, waiting for Mary Ellen to sign about twelve copies of some forms, she thought about herself and Arne. When one person in a couple liked the other one a great deal more, it was hard on both of them.

The pendulum clock on the wall had just chimed five times when Barry escorted Mary Ellen out of the inner office. "I guess we're ready to go," he told the others. "Mission accomplished. Your friend is now a wealthy woman."

"I hope you're all not just interested in me for my money," Mary Ellen joked. In reality, she felt a little strange about the check in her purse. She thought about the creases between Pres's father's eyes. He always seemed worried about something — and he was the richest man in Tarenton. Maybe this check of hers would turn out to be a mixed blessing.

"Come on, Mary Ellen," Angie laughed. "Stop worrying about your new image and let's go comb our hair. I saw a bathroom right near the front door." She practically yanked her down the corridor, leaving Barry and Pres standing together. "We'll meet you outside," she called as she closed the bathroom door behind them.

"Okay, Mary Ellen, come clean," Angie said sternly, leaning on the closed door. "You want to ditch Barry here and now — am I correct?"

Mary Ellen sighed and reached in her purse for her comb. When in doubt about something, it invariably helped her to know she looked good. "I guess. I mean, when I first met him, I was kind of wowed by all his credentials. But they don't cover up for the fact that he's, well, just plain dull."

Angie nodded, smiling over her friend's shoulder into the mirror opposite them. "I thought as much. You don't find Patrick dull, do you?"

Mary Ellen turned around suddenly. "I never have. I don't think I ever will, either." She missed him. Gone only half a day, and already she felt his loss.

"I rest my case," Angie said. "The best thing to do is tell Barry now. Don't just hide behind me and Pres for the rest of the trip. I mean, you can see the guy is dying to get you alone, and he seems so disappointed that you dragged two chaperones along."

"Maybe he'll just catch on as the evening progresses," Mary Ellen said hopefully.

Angie shook her head. "Do it. Tell him. Don't leave it to chance. Being honest is the nicest thing you could do — really."

"I suppose you're right," Mary Ellen sighed. "But tell me," she said, turning to her friend curiously. "You seem to be in a similar situation yourself. What's going on with you and Arne?"

Angie shrugged. "Beats me. I like going places with him, doing things with him. And needless to say, he's brilliant, and that kind of challenges me to think a little harder than I usually do. But. . . ." She shook her head, puzzled by her own feelings. If it was all so good, then why did she feel so ambivalent?

"But sparks don't fly when you look into his eyes," Mary Ellen finished her thought for her.

"Right. Except, for now, maybe I don't need a major forest fire. You, on the other hand, already have something burning. Why throw a bucket of cold water on it?" Taking the focus off herself was something Angie excelled at.

121

"I guess we both have some thinking to do."
Mary Ellen smiled, tucking her comb into the
pocket of her purse. "But we can't do it while
those two are waiting out in the parking lot."
They walked out together, arm in arm, wearing
the special smiles of friends who share something
important. The two guys, on the other hand, were
awkwardly shifting from foot to foot, clearly at a
loss for something to say.

"There you are!" Barry came toward them
as they approached. "Okay, next stop, Martrain
College," he grinned, guiding Mary Ellen over to
his Chevy. "You two follow us, okay?" He left
no room for argument, but quickly helped her
into the passenger seat. She gave Angie a nod as
they drove off, as if to say that she intended to
take charge of the situation before it was too late.

But as they walked around the campus, Mary
Ellen lost her impetus. She was too busy admir-
ing the new modern buildings and the incredible
athletic center, with its Olympic-sized pool; in-
door tennis and squash courts; four gyms; and
the sparkling clean lockers, with saunas, whirl-
pools, and massage rooms. By the time Barry
had completed the tour back at his dormitory
and introduced them all to his prelaw pals, it
seemed clear to Mary Ellen that it would be hard
to discuss their relationship on this particular
trip. And Barry had invited all his friends to
join them in the cafeteria for dinner, as though
he, too, needed a barricade of protection around
him. It was interesting, she thought, that Barry's
friends seemed so much like him. They were all

very earnest young men, none of whom had much of a sense of humor.

Eight of them grabbed a window table that faced the tree-lined quadrangle outside the cafeteria, and Barry volunteered to get Cokes for everyone while they sat around and decided which "gourmet" main course to order. The tallest guy in the group, a redhead named Pacer Lawrence, made sure that he sat next to Angie. She looked at Mary Ellen when the guy pulled up a chair between her and Pres, and the two of them exchanged knowing smiles.

"Joe, Dave, and Pacer — you guys take care of my Tarenton friends for a sec. I'll be right back," Barry told them. "Keep these cheerleaders occupied while I go get us something to drink." Barry seemed to feel comfortable leaving Mary Ellen in this group. None of his friends posed that much of a threat.

"Ah, you're a . . . a cheerleader, too?" Pacer asked Pres.

"And proud of it," Pres nodded casually. He was so used to getting ribbed about being a male cheerleader by now that he took it as a compliment. He just liked being different, even if it was *weird*-different.

"Well, when you kids grow up and go to college," Dave said patronizingly, "you will learn that basketball and football are not just fun and games that you jump around and cheer for."

"What do you mean?" Angie asked. "Thanks," she nodded to Barry when he placed a Coke in front of her.

"Oh, he's talking about point-shaving, I bet," Barry said as he took his seat. "Haven't you been reading about those college basketball teams that are in so much trouble for throwing games?"

"What are you talking about?" Mary Ellen demanded. Suddenly, her stomach was in a turmoil.

"Yeah, it's been in all the papers," Pacer nodded. "People place bets on who's going to win what games, see, and by how many points. It's not legal, but they do it anyway."

"And the teams know in advance how much they're supposed to win by," Dave continued. "Which means that a key player could be paid off *not* to make that many points. To shave points off his score."

"I've heard of it," Pres said.

Barry shrugged, shaking his head. "Cheating's everywhere now. If it's not on the playing field, it's in the classroom. Guys cheat on tests all the time, or write each other's papers for cash. Anyhow, you innocent kids have all that to look forward to."

"Or maybe everybody will clean up their act by the time these young ones are in college." Joe laughed sarcastically. The tone of his voice implied that he didn't believe this for a second.

The topic of cheating didn't come up again until the next morning, when Pres, Angie, and Mary Ellen were down in her uncle Roger's basement, working on their trio routine for halftime. The dance was grueling, hard work that demanded maximum physical ability and total concentration. By the time they'd gone over it four times, they were all exhausted.

"You don't think that's what's going on, do you?" Pres said finally, when the three of them sprawled on the floor, sweating and panting from dozens of backbends, cartwheels, and stag leaps.

"What?" Angie asked. She was too trusting to connect his words with the conversation of the previous night.

"Are you talking about point-shaving, Pres?" Mary Ellen demanded. "Because if you are, that's total nonsense. Ben wouldn't do that kind of thing. He's not made that way."

"Yeah, well what about Donny? He's been so burned that Ben's on the team, he's determined to show him up somehow. They've both been looking bad. So how else do you want to explain this?" Pres ticked off the possibilities on his fingers. "Say one of them got a hurt wrist and the other a twisted ankle, maybe? No, Coach would have noticed that. Just a string of bad luck? Too coincidental. Lack of morale — like falling off a horse once or twice and not being able to get back on? I don't think so."

"That's a terribly serious accusation," Mary Ellen said stiffly. "I hope you're ready to back it up. If not, it should stay right here in this room with the three of us."

Pres shook his head, then reached over to pull his chest down to his outstretched thighs. "I don't know. Maybe I am talking through my hat. In which case, I better shut up."

But over the next two days, as their stay in Mayville drew to a close, the topic was on each of their minds. That, and the question of what Mary Ellen was going to do about Barry. She

125

agreed to go out with him the last night of their stay, and their date was subdued, to say the least. She knew she couldn't keep up the pretense any longer.

"Well, have you thought about how you're going to invest that money?" Barry asked, when they had exhausted all other topics of conversation. "Because, you know, you've got lots of possibilities."

"No, actually. I've thought about long-term stuff, like college or a big trip, but I don't know exactly what to do with it now except put it in the bank."

"Hey, that's stupid. You can earn much more with other investment tools," he said eagerly, warming to his subject. "There's money markets and C.D.'s. I can get you some brochures from some of the new growth companies, too."

"Barry," Mary Ellen sighed, "I really appreciate all your help and everything, but — "

"But you just aren't interested . . . in me," Barry said dejectedly. "That's the whole deal, isn't it?"

"I. . . ." She was too flabbergasted by his outright statement to admit it. Was it really so obvious that all she wanted to do was get home to Patrick?

"Don't apologize," Barry said with a self-deprecating shrug. "I guess there's someone else. There was this cheerleader I was nuts about when I was in high school — she never went for me, though. The prettiest girls always have someone else by the time I meet them."

Mary Ellen's heart went out to him. "Hey,"

she said, covering his hand with hers, "you'll find someone. It may just take you a little while, that's all. But don't give up. Don't ever give up."

When he brought her back to her uncle's house, he gave her a quick kiss on the cheek. "It's been great knowing you, Mary Ellen," he said. She said good-bye with a lighter heart, feeling at once sorry that she'd had to hurt him and also relieved of the burden of his liking her too much.

Angie was right, she thought as she walked inside and listened to the sound of his car's engine die away in the distance. You have to be straight with people. Otherwise, you're cheating them. It was a good lesson to have learned. She couldn't wait to explain that to Patrick.

CHAPTER

11

W alt, Olivia, and Nancy had come up with a spectacular routine. It was so good and so well-rehearsed, in fact, that Ardith joked about breaking up the squad more often. It was true that Nancy went through her moves with a dazed look on her face, but she didn't let her concerns interfere with her work. She knew what she had to do, and she didn't want the other cheerleaders involved until she was absolutely sure. This responsibility was hers, and hers alone.

Ardith was still going on about how good they'd been. "I don't know. Give you some leeway, some time apart, and it generally creates havoc. This time, though, it worked fine. Neat, clean lines, nice execution. Olivia, that handspring off Walt's shoulders is perfectly death-defying."

"Yeah, one thing Livvy loves to do is scare

128

everybody to death," Walt laughed, giving his girl friend a gentle nudge between the ribs.

"All right, next group." Ardith turned to the other three. "Let's see how you did in Mayville."

Mary Ellen popped another cassette in the tape recorder, and she, Angie, and Pres gathered in a huddle at the end of the gym. The strong beat of reggae music blared, and the three of them came out dancing.

> "For a while,
> We'll make you smile.
> Today's the day we grab it.
> Get the bright brass ring,
> Hold tight and sing:
> We're the team to nab it.
>
> "Victory's ours,
> We're telling you,
> The championship is here.
> So watch us please,
> The day we'll seize,
> For Tarenton we cheer!"

Mary Ellen sprinted the length of the gym, then tucked in her knees and spun like a shining ball in the air, landing in Pres's outstretched arms and then, using Angie's back as a fulcrum, springing back onto the floor. The girls changed places and it was Angie's turn to catapult through space. The two girls on either side of Pres made a perfect, symmetrical picture as they finished the number together, the three of them sliding into splits on the floor.

Their colleagues couldn't resist — they leapt up and cheered.

"This is going to be the totally best halftime display we've ever had," Olivia said enthusiastically, pounding Angie on the back. "The crowd will go wild!"

"Yeah, if they can just forget the mess the basketball team will have made before we come out," Pres joked.

"All right, enough of that," Mary Ellen muttered. "We have to have enough spirit for the whole school, understand?"

"Yes, sir!" Pres promptly saluted, then picked up the discarded pompons that had been lying to one side of the gym and waved them in her face. "Rah-rah! Yay, team!" He made a face, then collapsed in a heap on the floor.

"Everybody up for the final numbers," Ardith announced, eager to get them back in line. "I know you're all worried about Saturday, and I am, too, but one thing I don't want to worry about is your performance. That means another hour of this right now and a long warm-up Saturday morning."

"It won't go too late, will it?" Nancy asked quietly. She hadn't spoken at all since they'd started working, and the other kids were suddenly struck by the hollow sound of her voice.

"Let's start at ten. That way we can get in three good hours of work before we knock off," Ardith suggested. "And after that, I want you all to go home and take afternoon naps."

"Naps!" Walt shrieked. "You want us to take naps!" He dissolved in laughter, repeating the

130

word *naps* incredulously as Olivia tried to get him to shut up.

"Do what you like," Ardith shrugged. "Just don't go out and run around all afternoon. I want you rested and ready to go promptly at eight. Okay, back to work!"

The kids did some aerial work on the mini-tramp, and then Mary Ellen led them all in a run-through. The "Hello," "Pride," and "Tiger" cheers were ones they could practically do in their sleep, but they kept polishing, kept moving. Each of them wanted desperately to try to over-come the disaster they all felt was imminent.

"I'm famished," Angie said as they trailed back to the lockers at the end of practice. "I simply cannot go home without something in my stomach. Who's up for Pizza Pete's?"

"Me!" Pres nodded immediately. "What about you, Mary Ellen?"

"Ah, no thanks. I think I'll pass." Mary Ellen figured that if she timed it just right, she could run into Patrick finishing his garbage route for the day. Since there was another day of reading week left, she wouldn't run into him at school, and the only other way to get hold of him would be to go to his house, something she felt funny about doing.

Walt and Olivia agreed to come along and, after a long moment's hesitation, Nancy said she'd come, too. She seemed to have a great deal on her mind, but nobody pressed her for details.

The group assembled after their showers out in the parking lot, and Pres, with Nancy in the passenger seat of his Porsche, began the trip to the mall in a driving snow. Walt, Olivia, and Angie followed after him in the Jeep.

They were not terribly surprised to discover that Pizza Pete's was nearly empty. Everyone who had stuck around the restaurant seemed to be watching out the windows carefully, wondering how bad the storm was going to get and whether they should make a quick getaway while there was still time.

"I was watching TV this morning while I got dressed," Angie volunteered to Walt as they all assembled at a window table. "That show your parents did on corruption in the high schools was really something." She turned around to see Pres marching proudly back from the counter carrying what Pete called his "Monster Pizza" — a giant round of bread, tomato sauce, cheese, anchovies, mushrooms, pepperoni, sausage, and artichokes.

"Yeah, wasn't it?" Walt agreed. "Never thought old Dad and Mom had it in them to cover hard issues like cheating in school."

"You know, it's weird," Angie went on, peering out the window into the storm. "When the three of us were in Mayville, we had dinner with these college guys who were talking about the exact same thing." She did not mention the private discussion they'd had later about Ben and Donny. She agreed with Mary Ellen that it was completely unfair to start second-guessing anybody without proof.

"Do you think. . . ?" Olivia began. Then she shook her head and took a large bite of pizza.

"What?" Nancy asked nervously.

"C'mon, Livvy, I think we should get this all out in the open," Walt urged her. "The squad ought to know what I'm going to do on Saturday."

But even as he spoke, the door to the restaurant opened, and six very wet, very cold people came rushing in, their hair and shoulders powdered with white.

"All right, Pete," Johnny Bainbridge called out, pulling the long scarf off his neck. "Let's have some service around here! Vannie, what do you want on your pizza?" One of his four buddies took their order and went up to the counter to tell Pete, as the other three sat laughing and comparing notes about the practice they'd just come from.

Vanessa, a perfect paragon of high fashion even in her snowy condition, slid easily into the booth opposite the cheerleaders' table, giving them all an appraising look and a nod that said, so I'm here with the Garrison captain and his friends. What are you going to do about it?

"Hello, boys and girls," she offered in her husky voice. "Nice weather we're having, isn't it?" She shook her dark hair, and gleaming droplets of water sprayed Nancy, who was sitting nearest to her. Nancy wiped her cheek as she gave Vanessa a look. "Johnny, you know all my school friends, don't you? You see before you the very spirit of Tarenton High — the cheering squad that's going to lead our team onto victory this Saturday."

Johnny chuckled meanly, slipping an arm around Vanessa's waist. "You guys really think you have a prayer anymore? Hey, I've been at some of your games. That Northfield disaster was really something. What happened to Donny Parrish, anyhow? He get his feet stuck in cement?"

"You know. . . ." Pres was struggling to keep himself calm. "It's one thing to boast, Bainbridge. It's another to smear the opposition."

"Oh, Pres, dear, don't be a sore loser." Vanessa got up, delicately lifting Johnny's arm off her, and sauntered over to them. "I'm just as disappointed as you all are that Tarenton has been doing so badly. But face it, Garrison can't be beat right now. Johnny is playing better than he ever has, and his backup people are just great. I'm afraid you're going to lose that bet. But it's all right if you can't pay up. I could always collect some other way," she added with a suggestive smile.

Vanessa almost never failed to turn Pres on, and there had been times when her compliance and pure delight in snaring him had resulted in some heavy sessions. But now he was mad. Her smarmy behavior was getting to him. "Forget it, Van," he barked. "I've got the funds available. A loan from a friend. I won't need it, though."

"Oh?" A twinkle of interest sparked in her dark eyes. "And which one of you is helping him out? Nancy, I bet it's you. Or is it your boyfriend?" She laughed, thrilled with her supposition. "Why how nice of Ben, to pay off the bet you made on him, Pres. Yes, of course it must be him. After all, I saw those darling fur mittens he bought Nancy. The earrings, too, right?" She put out a finger toward the opal hanging from the other girl's ear, but Nancy tossed her head and moved away before Vanessa could touch her. "And that car of his! An Isuzu — you hardly see any of those around. Must have cost a pretty penny."

"Vanessa," Angie cut in, "could you just leave us in peace? I'm trying to digest my meal, and it's perfectly impossible to do that while I'm listening to your stupid insinuations."

"Good idea," Walt agreed, turning to swipe another slice of the now cold pizza off their platter.

"Well, certainly!" Vanessa got out of her seat, and, slipping her arm through Johnny's, started away toward the other side of the room. "Bring the pizza, will you, guys?" she called to the four Garrison players at their booth. "We're not wanted over here."

The five cheerleaders turned back to their meal, considerably more downhearted than they had been before Vanessa's appearance. There was something about her that put a very large damper on things.

"You know," Nancy said quietly as the others picked at the food in silence, "she could be right."

"About what?" Walt asked. He looked over at Vanessa who was giggling wildly over Johnny's attempt to stuff an entire slice of pizza into his mouth.

Nancy looked as though she was going to say something, then hesitated. "About Ben having a lot of money lately. The last time we dated, we always went dutch. Now he won't let me pay for anything."

Pres shrugged. "Maybe he just got generous all of a sudden."

"About who's responsible for all our losses," Walt interjected, getting back to the subject that obsessed him, "Vanessa's barking up the wrong basketball player."

"Walt. . . ." Livvy gave him a warning look.

"No, c'mon, we're all in this together," Walt said. "I think it's important that we discuss it."

"Well, what?" Angie prodded.

"Oh, I think we're making too much of this," Olivia stated.

"No! No, we're not. I'm convinced it's all Donny's fault," Walt went on more quickly. "And he's doing it deliberately. I have the whole thing figured out."

"That's insane. Why would Donny do a thing like that to his own school?" Angie demanded. "I mean, last year, he would have killed to make Ben look inept. And to make Garrison lose. It could just be bad luck," she finished.

"Or it could be money," Nancy blurted out.

The others just stared at her, shocked into silence by Nancy's statement. They had no idea that she was not talking about Donny at all.

"Wow! I never thought of *that*," Walt said. "I mean, I was thinking that Donny Parrish has worked his butt off to get to be first-string center on the Varsity team, and then his worst rival comes in and bumps him to second. That could make anyone crazy. But money — there's another motive." He rubbed his hands together, sensing that his plot was thickening.

Pres dropped his head into his hands and

leaned his elbows on the table. "That is what I was talking about, Ange. Remember that business about point-shaving?"

"But . . . that's incredible!" Angie was horrified.

"Listen, you guys," Walt said in a hushed whisper, "the guilty party is coming out in the open — I hope before the Garrison game ever begins on Saturday."

Nancy shook her head and got up from the table. "Pres, take me home, would you? I promised I wouldn't be late." Nancy's face was white, her eyes showing the anxiety she had kept so well hidden from her squad members. She hated herself for waiting so long, but up until now, she'd refused to believe that the real culprit in all this was Ben. All those gifts, all that cockiness about being able to snatch victory from the jaws of Garrison. But it had to be true — didn't it? What other explanation could there be?

Nancy sat beside Pres in the car, doubting her own good judgment. Everyone had warned her against Ben, and yet she'd gone out with him — a second time — because she was so thrilled that he had wanted her. He had walked into school, become king of the roost, and selected Nancy out of the waiting crowd.

But now she just felt sorry for him, disappointed in him and in herself. He wasn't a king after all. He was just a jerk.

Pres, sensing Nancy's despondent mood, half turned to her. The windshield wipers beat on heavily, a steady metronome in the dark car. "It's not that awful. We've won before. Ben could just pull it off for us this time, despite what Donny does." He could see how hard it was for her to admit that something she'd had such high hopes for had fallen apart, right before her eyes. "Maybe we'll come out on top," he said quietly.

"I hope so. I'm still holding out a chance," Nancy sighed.

"Yeah," Pres laughed, trying to cheer her up. "And if you go around with this long face before the game, you're going to be real embarrassed when we win."

"I'd be *thrilled* to be embarrassed," she said quietly, thinking of the confrontation she would have to have with Ben. She tucked herself into her big down parka and zipped it the rest of the way up to her chin with a determined gesture. "I just don't want to be right."

She would do it Saturday, before the game. Maybe she could scare him into winning.

CHAPTER

Mary Ellen hated driving in snow. Ever since that awful night of the accident, when she'd been hit broadside by a van, she was extra careful when she went out at night. And bad weather made her super cautious. But she had no choice right now. She had to talk to Patrick.

Funny, she thought, as she drove slowly, following the gleam of her fog lights through the driving snow. *I was on my way to make up with Patrick that night, too.* Would she spend the rest of her life having these lousy misunderstandings with him and then realizing she'd been rotten and have to apologize? Maybe this was simply the nature of their relationship — sometimes bad, sometimes good, always challenging, interesting, and, well . . . sexy. She smiled to herself as she thought of Patrick's wide, sensual mouth, his strong hands with the long fingers that knew just how to touch.

She went around the lake once, figuring that it would be smarter to start with the end of his route and work backwards. There was still some light in the sky, despite the storm, and she found that if she stayed directly behind the car in front of her, she didn't have too much of a problem. But then the traffic thinned out and she didn't have anyone to follow. She made herself slow down to thirty miles an hour as she took the road back toward the center of Tarenton.

It felt like hours before she reached the end of the small residential district, and yet she could see from the clock on the dashboard that it was only seven. It was dark now, and her headlights seemed to taunt her, illuminating nothing before her but the ever-present white that cleared only for a brief moment as the windshield wipers took a swipe at it. Then, immediately, her vision was fogged once again.

There were a few more cars around now, though, and that was a relief. At this rate, Mary Ellen thought, she wouldn't get home till ten, and her mother would be worried sick that she'd been in another car crash. This is stupid, she decided after another futile tour of the district. I'm going straight back to my house.

Then the pavement seemed to slip out from under her and she grabbed the steering wheel as her heart lurched. "Turn in the direction of the skid!" she said aloud, trying to make the car behave. She slid in a half circle as traffic came to a dead stop around her. She could feel the pulse banging away in her right temple as she fought to gain control of the steering — and finally won. She manuevered the car over to the curb, parked it, and turned the ignition key. Then she closed her eyes and rested her head on top of the steering wheel. Whiteness surrounded her.

It would have been worse than dumb to keep going — it would have been suicidal. The car would be fine right here overnight, and she could get her dad to drop her off on his bus route in the morning so that she could pick it up.

Pulling her scarf up around her head, Mary Ellen got out of the car and locked it, shouldered her duffle bag, and started off on foot. She was about six blocks from the bus that would take her back to her neighborhood, and was enormously grateful that she'd worn her old scuffed, flat-heeled boots. Not waterproof, of course, but better than nothing.

She began to walk, squinting against the onslaught of heavy snow that flew in her eyes and nose. This was really loony, actually. Romance was nothing but trouble, when it came down to it. It brought you not only heartache, but lack of transportation, wet feet, and probably a cold in the morning. Was it all worth it? she wondered as she trudged along.

And then she collided head-on with someone going in the opposite direction.

"Oh, sorry — " she began.

"Why don't you watch — ?" he said, and then, grabbing her by the shoulders, he hugged her to him. "You little idiot," Patrick declared. "What in the name of Pete are you doing out in this storm?"

She was so happy to see him, she threw her

141

arms around his waist and pressed him closer, feeling the warmth of his body right through her wet clothes. "Just a stroll before dinner," she joked. "You never know who you might run into." As she looked up into his dark, concerned eyes, she knew he had forgiven her. And yet, she also knew she had to be worthy of that forgiveness.

"How about a lift?" she asked. "I mean, I don't *mind* the walk, but seeing as how it's getting a bit blustery. . . ." She grinned at him, then asked, "Where's the truck?"

"I didn't think rich girls rode in garbage trucks," Patrick said carefully, his arms sheltering her light body, so thinly dressed. But even as he spoke, he was steering her toward the white truck that seemed like a piece of the storm frozen right there on the street.

She didn't say a word, but let him help her up into the cab. They sat together in silence, cozy and safe in their dark, warm lair, protected from the howling wind. Then she pulled the scarf off her head and began toweling her hair dry. The golden strands fell to her shoulders, loose and curling, and Patrick could only marvel at how totally beautiful she was, and how completely and utterly hooked he was on Mary Ellen Kirkwood — no matter what she did or said to him.

"Well, you know what they say, Patrick," she sighed, leaning her head back against the seat. "Rich girls are born, not made."

"Is that so? Did your lawyer friend tell you that?" he asked, somewhat bitterly.

"Patrick, please. That guy — well, he was a

142

nice guy, but nothing special to me."

Patrick sighed and looked down at his fingernails. "I've heard you say that before. I told you, Mary Ellen, I really can't take this juggling act of yours anymore. I mean it."

She saw that she was losing him, and it had never seemed more important to her to have him back. "You shouldn't have to take it. I'm a louse. But I don't want to be, Patrick. And maybe this time I've learned something. Maybe I don't have to be." She bit her lip, thinking about all the times she'd left him for someone who seemed better, brighter, more special. They never were. "Barry never did anything but bore me — honest. You were right about what makes people who they are. A suit and tie, or a job in somebody's law office doesn't make a person a person. But you know me, always confusing what's on the outside with what's on the inside. I learn — eventually. And I know what I have in you, which is really and truly exceptional — no matter what you're wearing."

He thought about that a minute, not looking at her. "You really don't think the two thousand is going to change what's on the inside of you?"

"I don't think anybody changes overnight, not unless they were awfully shallow to begin with. You may think a lot of bad things about me, but you have to admit that there's a core of something or other there that won't go away. I don't feel any different, despite the money." She giggled a little, as though she were embarrassed about it. "I don't even know what I'm going to do with it. It'll probably just sit in the bank earning interest like the money you earn from working your garbage route, and I'll never even use it. I won't seem any richer than I was before."

"Well, that's pretty dumb," he said practically. "You ought to have a party, at least, or take a guy out to dinner."

She turned her head languidly, smiling at him shyly. "If I asked you, would you go to dinner with me, Patrick?"

"You wouldn't even have to ask." He brought his head close to hers and leaned in slowly, savoring the smell of her hair and the delicious cold radiating off her cheeks and mouth. Then he kissed her, and they were both lost in the kiss, the storm raging outside nothing to compare with the one that bound them both together.

It snowed most of Friday, and the weather gave Nancy just the opportunity she needed. She and Ben had decided to spend the day together in the library studying, which was basically what they did. Ben studied his trigonometry and history; Nancy studied Ben.

"If it's nice tomorrow, maybe we could go over to my house before the game and just hang out," Ben said, just before he left to go home for dinner. He looked slightly punchy from the unaccustomed activity of cracking the books. "I want to work on the car awhile, okay?"

"That'd be great. I'd love to spend some time alone with you, Ben," she said coyly, looking at him from under her long, dark eyelashes.

Suddenly, his head bobbed up. Nancy had been so standoffish with him for a while, he couldn't quite believe what he'd just heard. The other kids at their library table had just packed up their books as she reached across and stroked his hand. There was a hidden message in her eyes that he kept trying to read, but couldn't exactly make out. "Well, great! Sure. What time do I pick you up?" he asked eagerly.

"I have practice from ten to one. Then we can spend the day and go to the game together later." She raised her hand to his cheek and slowly stroked his face. The message in her eyes was much clearer now. "How about it?" she smiled.

"Hey!" he exclaimed, scooping his books up under one arm and Nancy under the other. "I have this definite feeling that tomorrow is going to be a really heavy-duty day."

He didn't know the half of it.

Saturday, the skies cleared. The sun was out and everything had begun to melt by the time the cheerleaders assembled for their morning workout. Ardith kept at them, making them go through routines over and over, yelling at them to keep those smiles on their faces, to put more energy into the impossible jumps and pyramids they had grown used to by now.

Ardith stopped them before one, feeling that they might get stale if they worked anymore. But before she dismissed them, she sat them down in a semicircle in front of her.

"I don't usually bother with pep talks," she said, stalking the length of the gym, "but I feel I have to try and do something about what's going on inside you. It's not just your bodies, the outside, that's involved, you know."

Mary Ellen smiled, but her coach couldn't have known why.

"I would be the last person in the world to suggest that you should prepare yourselves for a loss tonight, because that's not how I operate. But I want to remind you that winning or losing the basketball game has nothing to do with your own personal victory. You can still be the best cheering squad in the league. What the players on the teams do doesn't affect that. So go out there and win — for yourselves. Don't even think about the play-offs. You're what counts out there, no one else."

She put her hands on her hips, and gave the squad a fleeting smile. "See you tonight. And get some rest," she called after Walt, who was already halfway toward the door.

"Naps! Naps!" he called back over his shoulder.

Nancy beat the other girls back to the locker room and was dressed and out in record time, pausing only to say brief good-byes to her friends. She didn't have much time now.

Ben was waiting outside, the Isuzu still running. He had on a black and white biker's cap, turned around backwards, and his black corduroy jacket. Nancy saw him before he saw her, and she noticed that he seemed very preoccupied, fiddling with the buttons on his jacket like a person who feels edgy, anxious, pent up inside. All right, it was up to her now. All she had to do was get him to be honest. She hadn't a clue as to how she was going to do that.

"Well, are we ready?" she said cheerily. He

started when he heard her voice, and then he had on his confident face again, the one she knew so well.

"Hey, babe, we are as ready as we'll ever be." Ben grinned. His hand pressed the small of her back as he helped her into the car, but she didn't protest or move out of his grasp. Let him think she was really interested, that when they were alone at his house anything might happen. She was nervous, but she had to do this. It was for the good of the whole school.

The fresh snow made all of Tarenton sparkle, especially the lake and its surrounding trees. Ben lived way out on Fable Point, past Pres's house, in a really deluxe palace. Nancy's mother called it pretentious.

Nancy thought the place was a hoot. Lots of glass and chrome and a spiral staircase that went right up through the center of it. There was a double fireplace in the living room with a window on either side of it, so you could watch the snow come down and the fire go up at the same time. The eat-in kitchen was equipped with everything from microwaves to butcher-block counters to hanging hooks for the copper pots and pans that were Mrs. Adamson's pride and joy.

They had just zoomed up the drive and parked outside the garage when a white Sting Ray pulled up at the curb a few yards down from the house. The driver honked his horn and Ben looked back through his rearview mirror to see who it was. Suddenly, his face changed. Nancy thought he looked very annoyed about something.

"Darn. Not *now*," Ben muttered.

147

"What is it?" she asked.

"Look, stay here a minute, will you? I just have to take care of some business. Then I'm all yours." He planted a kiss on her lips, then chucked her playfully under the chin, but she could see that he was still mad and trying not to show it.

She stayed in the car and watched as Ben hurried down the drive, looking like someone was after him. Whose Sting Ray was that, anyway? She didn't recognize it, and she pretty much knew all the hot cars around school. She didn't want to appear too interested, just in case he glanced back, so as she turned around, she pretended to be busy with something in the backseat.

She could see the person in the passenger seat clearly, and the fact that it was Vanessa Barlow didn't surprise her in the least. Well, of course. Whenever there was trouble, there was Vanessa. And who had she been playing around with lately? Johnny Bainbridge, from Garrison. Yes, she recognized his unmistakable shock of curly red hair as he leaned out of the window on the driver's side to talk to Ben. Johnny Bainbridge! That would explain why she didn't know the car.

Ben stood leaning over, shaking his head as he talked with Johnny. Then she saw Johnny press a brown envelope into his hand. Ben shook his head again and passed the envelope back, but Johnny just laughed and threw the package at Ben. It landed in the snow with a thump. Then the Sting Ray backed up fast, nearly all the way down the block. Ben watched it for a second, then picked up the envelope and jammed it into his jacket pocket. After another minute, he walked back up the drive. Nancy quickly opened her purse and immersed herself in her mother's less-than-fascinating grocery list.

"All done?" she asked casually.

"Right. C'mon inside. You cold enough for me to make a fire?" He was all over her as soon as she was inside the front door. His tall body bent over her, as he didn't wait for an answer but instead, covered her face and neck with kisses. Nancy felt sick, but she didn't pull away. She could feel the envelope pressing against her right cheek.

"How about that fire? Then we can get real comfy. Are you sure your parents won't be home this afternoon?" she whispered, leaning back to unzip his jacket. He pulled away from her as though she'd hit him. But the funny thing was, she didn't hate him. She just pitied him.

"Yeah, right. Let me put our coats in the hall closet and I'll start it." His hand on hers felt clammy, and he quickly wiped it on his pants leg.

"Here. I'll hang them up." She shrugged out of her parka and tried to take his jacket, but he wouldn't let go.

"Forget it, Nance. I'll — " He yanked it away from her and moved so abruptly that the jacket fell to the floor. The envelope hadn't even been sealed. A bunch of twenty-dollar bills lay scattered on the creamy beige carpet.

"Oh, God." Nancy couldn't look at him. "I was afraid of that." Her mind reeled with the awful truth: Ben had taken a bribe from Johnny. That's why Tarenton had lost all those games. That's why they were going to lose against Garrison tonight.

"Nancy, let me explain. I — " His self-confidence was gone, his rugged, dangerous looks for once softer, more vulnerable. He hadn't made a move to pick up the money on the floor.

"Oh, *please,*" she said sarcastically. "Explain away."

"I didn't want this cash. I told Johnny the whole deal was off last week, but he wouldn't believe me. He'd already given me fifty bucks on account. That's how I bought you the mittens and earrings and records. I took a loan from my dad to pay Johnny back and I tried to make him see — "

"I can see you tried real hard." Nancy's voice was cold, cutting like steel.

"Nancy, I gave him back the fifty last week. But he kept after me, kept reminding me about all I owed Garrison. I'd been there three years, and at Tarenton only a few months, so in the beginning, I thought, Well, why not? Johnny took up a collection," he laughed bitterly. "He got all the players at his school and some guys from the other schools to chip in. The pot was two hundred for me if I lost Tarenton the championship."

"So that's why we bombed out on all those games. You did it deliberately."

"No. That's not true. I was just so uptight, I couldn't play well. I made a mistake, I admit it. I never should have gone along with those guys."

"But you did," she said with a hollow laugh. Nancy had never felt such contempt for another human being. It was hard for her to remain in the

150

same room with him. "You're a creep, Ben," was all she said. Then she started for the door.

"I did it for you," he said quietly. "I didn't want to blow it between us this time. See, when I got to Tarenton and we started going out again, it was just fun and games, another conquest. But then I got to know you better, and I realized you weren't like anyone I'd ever dated. I honestly liked you . . . *like* you," he corrected himself. "I've never felt that way about any girl before."

She turned around, wanting to stay angry with him. "You're not getting off the hook that easy. You still don't have any excuse for even thinking about taking bribes."

"No, you're right. I don't. Look, I thought this was a crummy deal way back at the beginning. Remember the scrimmage with Garrison when I was so late? You had to call me and tell me to get moving. I said I'd fallen asleep and didn't know what time it was, but the truth is, I figured if I didn't show up, I wouldn't have to deal with the game."

Nancy listened, but wasn't convinced.

"I'm not just making excuses, Nance. I'm not going to take this cash. . . ." He looked at the pile of bills on the floor lamely, and she turned away from him.

"I just got it into my head that buying you things was the only way to make sure you stayed my girl," he went on desperately. "I know it sounds dumb, but some girls are like that. You treat them nice enough and they want to be with you."

She couldn't believe what she was hearing.

151

"Don't you know anything about me at all?" she asked incredulously. Then, deliberately, she unscrewed the posts of her opal earrings and removed them. "These are yours," she said, holding them out to him. "Please, take them back."

"But, Nancy — "

"I'm not like that. I don't care about *things* when they're bought with blood money." When he wouldn't take them from her, she sat them down on the end table and walked away.

He winced. "I know that . . . now. But I didn't before. I was wrong, Nancy. I guess it doesn't matter now, because you're going to hate me regardless of what I do." He bent down and picked up the money, looking about as hopeless as she'd ever seen anyone look.

"Take me home, will you, Ben?" she asked coldly. "I don't think we have anything more to talk about."

She had intended to ask him about the game, to plead with him if need be, to try every trick in the book to get him to win for Tarenton. But she was just too disgusted with the whole idea of Ben's cheating to get more involved than she already was. As for whether they could still win tonight, well, one look at Ben's face told her that now that was impossible. He'd taken the cash, and that meant he was on *their* side. She could never trust him again.

CHAPTER

13

Walt barreled into the parking lot a full hour early. He'd persuaded Olivia that they had to get to school when the basketball players did, even though the cheerleaders didn't have to start warming up much before seven.

"I'll get him right before the game, see," he explained to her as they raced up the steps to Tarenton High's front door. "Donny wouldn't dare throw the game after I've confronted him."

Olivia gave him a look. "Walt, you're not going to accomplish anything this way. Really, just forget it. If we lose, we lose. You heard what Mrs. Engborg said yesterday. Just resign yourself to it and you'll feel better."

"My magic tape recorder is going to convince Donny to change his mind. I can do it — I know it." Walt pounded his fist into his thigh and started for the boys' locker room. "See you in half an hour. I will succeed!" he called out as the door closed behind him.

Olivia smiled. She loved the guy a lot, but he was out of his mind.

"Listen, we can up the score after halftime if need be," Chuck Maxwell was saying to a couple of his teammates as Walt pushed through the swinging doors of the locker room. "As long as we don't count on Adamson or Parrish pulling us through, we can make those extra baskets and do it to Garrison."

"Yeah, you and who else, Maxwell?" asked a disgusted Hank Vreewright.

Walt put on his white sweater with the red stripes down the arm and the matching red pants. Then he slapped on his headphones as though they were part of his uniform, holding them to his ears every time a word was spoken from the other end of the bench. When Pres walked in and said hello, Walt didn't pay any attention, but kept fiddling with his cassette player, stopping and starting it over and over.

"What's going on?" Pres asked, when he didn't get a response the third time he nudged Walt.

But then Donny walked in, followed a couple seconds later by Ben, and Walt was off in the stratosphere once again, getting more annoyed by the minute with the dials and buttons on his tape recorder. Pres shrugged and walked away to get dressed.

"Machines!" Walt finally exclaimed, ripping the headphones off with a dramatic gesture.

"What's the matter, Manners? The squawk box won't squawk?" Donny laughed, as he unbuttoned his shirt and reached into his duffle bag for his uniform.

Walt threw down the tape recorder and headphones with a curse, took a breath, and went right up to Donny. The basketball player towered over him.

"Okay," Walt nodded grimly. "All right. My tape recorder's jammed, no problem." He narrowed his eyes and grunted, working up the steam for what he was about to say. "Look, Parrish, we know you're the one responsible for Tarenton's lousy performance. You were jealous about Adamson coming on board, and you've been messing up ever since. But this is the big one, right? This is the one that counts. So just come off it. We get the point already."

Donny looked at Pres, then at his teammates. "Anybody know what this guy's ranting about?"

Pres shook his head. He clearly didn't want any part of this.

"I had you on tape at the Northfield game, Parrish, saying you couldn't go through with it. Don't try to worm out of that one. And I was going to tape you again when you started muttering, but the darn recorder wouldn't cooperate. I know you're guilty."

"Oh, come off it, Manners." Donny dismissed him as though he were an annoying gnat at a summer picnic and turned away.

Ben stood at the opposite end of the bench, slowly putting on his singlet and shorts. He listened to the exchange between Walt and Donny, blank-faced.

"Go on, deny it!" Walt pestered. He followed

155

Donny down the line of lockers to the water fountain. The other guys just stood around taking it all in. "I got you on tape, for Pete's sake!"

"Yeah? What'd I say? I said I can't go through with it? What does that mean, Manners?" Donny sneered. "I guess it means I can't save a whole game when someone else is trying to throw it." He turned and gave Ben a stare so intense it made everyone else in its path cringe. Ben, ignoring him, began doing some deep knee bends.

"Okay, boys, everybody ready?" The sound of Coach Cooley's voice stopped what might have turned into a fight. "We can do it to Garrison tonight — I know we can!" His pep and vigor sounded artificial, and all the boys picked up on it.

"So, let's go over the strategies, okay? Adamson, you're first-string, so you're starting."

"Sure, Coach," Ben said, but his mind was elsewhere. "Can you give me just a sec before you talk plays? There's something I have to do." He took a rolled-up T-shirt from his duffle and marched purposefully out the door of the locker room.

Coach Cooley shrugged, as if to excuse any kind of temperament in his star player. He didn't know if they still had a prayer, but if they did, it was up to Ben.

Walt sank dejectedly onto one of the benches as the coach began talking. "It's no good, Pres," he said sadly to his friend.

"You mean I'm going to lose my bet with Vanessa," Pres nodded.

"Looks that way." Walt sighed.

They met the girls fifteen minutes later in the practice room, and it would have been hard to say who was the most depressed of the crew. The bright Tarenton uniforms, the neat short skirts with their white pleats peeking out from the crimson folds, did nothing to lighten the girls' looks. Mary Ellen was the only one wearing a smile, but that had everything to do with Patrick and nothing to do with the game that was about to be played.

Nancy might, in fact, have felt the lowest of the group. She lay on the floor doing leg lifts, staring up at the ceiling, wishing she could say something. She had thought about it all afternoon, from the time Ben dropped her off at her house, but she couldn't bring herself to confide the awful secret to her squad members. Taking money to fix games was illegal, and much as she despised Ben now, she knew she was incapable of getting anyone — even him — into that much trouble.

"All of you, look alive," Mary Ellen said after she had gone through the roster of cheers. "We're going to be magnificent, even if the game's a bust. Let's go!"

She hustled them out the door and down the hall to the gym. She could hear Mrs. Oetjen, the principal, greeting the crowd. She could see the basketball teams lined up next to the doors — Tarenton on one side, Garrison on the other. And then she heard the cue for the squad to start, and she quickly turned to the other five.

"We're going to win!" she said in a fierce whisper as she led the way, bursting through the gym door.

> "Tarenton fights hard — *fight, fight, fight!*
> Always looking good, we're *right, right, right!*
> We've got pride, we've got grace,
> We can land the other guys
> Flat on their face!
> *Yay, team!*"

She did a double somersault and spun through the arch that Olivia and Angie made with their handstands. The two boys lifted her and Nancy high in the air and for a moment, she felt that elation that always comes before a win. The truth of the matter was, even as she smiled at Patrick, who was snapping pictures across the gym like crazy, she had a strange intuition that they really could win, despite what Donny or Ben might pull.

The crowd went wild as the two teams raced in, Garrison first because they were the visitors. One of the referees read off the names and positions of the players, and there were rousing cheers from the bleachers reserved for Garrison.

"And now, from Tarenton High, the starting line-up!" yelled the referee. "Center, Ben Adamson! Forward, Hank Vreewright! Forward, Chuck Maxwell! Guard, Andrew Poletti! Guard, Pete Raines!" He announced each player in turn, and the Tarenton Pompon Squad went wild, giving their all each time a new name was called off.

"This isn't going to be a pretty sight," Walt sighed, as he took his place next to Mary Ellen at the sidelines for the opening of the game. Nancy was chewing her fingernails; Pres looked pale with worry.

Ben stepped up to the center with Johnny Bainbridge for the tip-off. The referee tossed the ball high in the air, and Ben hit it hard, sending it halfway across the court. But by the time Andrew Poletti had it, Ben was right beside him, waiting for the pass. He took it easily from Andrew, who bounced it to him as he eluded the Garrison guard. Then, as though it were the easiest thing in the world, he dunked it into the basket.

Johnny Bainbridge snatched the ball on the turnover, dribbling it the length of the court. No one could manage to get it away from him. He passed it to one of his teammates, who dropped it, leaving it free for Ben. Ben went for the lay-up, but as the ball left his hand, one of the Garrison guards bumped Ben's arm. He missed the shot and the ref called a foul. "Two free throws," he yelled.

Ben took his place at the line and looped the ball in the air. It spun around the rim and fell through. The crowd cheered deliriously, and the sound got louder as Ben made the second basket. Mary Ellen took the opportunity to lead the squad in a quick "Pride" cheer. Nancy watched unbelieving as the ball got into play again and Ben scored three times in a row, easily upping the Tarenton ante.

The rest of the guys on the team caught the fire from Ben's enthusiasm and tightened their defense. Although Johnny Bainbridge was doing a terrific job, he and his teammates couldn't seem to hammer a wedge in the Tarenton flanks. They were so geared up, so alive with the taste of victory, that nothing could stop them.

Garrison didn't score on their next two trips down the court, but the third time down, the tables turned. Suddenly Johnny was everywhere, leaping into the air, scoring hook shots, reverse lay-ups, and alley-oops at every turn.

Coach Cooley began looking worried, and called a time-out. He put Donny in for Ben. "Not that I don't have faith in you, kid," he said to his star center. "I just want you to stay fresh, is all." Ben didn't protest, and sat calmly on the bench, watching the proceedings.

Nancy caught his eye across the court just before the halftime break. He seemed to be as sure of himself now as he'd ever been, and he wasn't ashamed of anything. She looked at him wonderingly, unable to figure out what was going on. He was winning for Tarenton! He was winning on purpose!

Tarenton had a two-point lead before halftime, and Donny upped the score by three just as the buzzer sounded. There was so much cheering going on in the bleachers, Mary Ellen couldn't even be heard as she led Pres and Angie into the center of the court for the first of the two trio numbers.

"I don't get it," Walt said to Nancy and Olivia as they watched their squad members dancing and leaping — for joy, this time. "I was sure we were going to lose."

Olivia stepped on his foot. "You're not supposed to say that."

"I know, but, they're so . . . so *good*! Donny and Ben both."

Nancy was silent. She was starting to feel that she had treated Ben pretty badly. Of course, it wasn't over yet. Maybe part of the deal was throwing the game in the second half. That way, it wouldn't look as suspicious.

Walt, Olivia, and Nancy stepped to the center for their trio, and they performed with the same energy as the first group. Ben couldn't take his eyes off Nancy. She was light, she was air — she was everything he'd ever wanted in a girl. The only problem was, she wasn't his anymore.

The players assembled for the second half, and this time it seemed to be a one-on-one match between Ben and Johnny. Both of them played all out, scoring in every conceivable position. The score was 46–44, Tarenton leading. The two boys were all over the court, not even bothering to pass to the other players. Johnny made a twenty-five foot shot and got three points. Ben grabbed the ball on the turnover and made a successful hook shot. Johnny managed to get it away from him, but then he double-dribbled, giving Ben another two points for the sky shot he made when the ball was put into play again. He and Johnny were neck and neck, each trying to outdo the other with his pyrotechnics.

The game wound down for the finish, and incredibly, the score was tied, 59 all. The cheerleaders were hoarse from yelling their approval, and everyone in the bleachers was on his feet when Ben snatched the ball and ran the length of the court with it, eluding his defender. There were only ten seconds to go. He jumped, and the ball got away from him, but he knocked the ball away as a Garrison player was dribbling. Ben recovered the ball, and then turning toward his own basket, he stopped, leaping into the air. He seemed to hang there in space as the ball left his hand. The buzzer sounded. The ball circled the rim, teetering precariously before falling through the hoop.

The noise threatened to blow the roof off the Tarenton gym. The crowd was wild, pouring out of the stands to embrace the exhausted players. Mary Ellen, Pres, and Angie were hugging each other; Walt and Olivia pounded each other on the back.

And the most amazing sight, the one that got the crowd going all over again, was the one of Donny Parrish walking over to Ben Adamson and sticking out his hand. Ben hesitated just for a moment, and then he shook it. And he kept on shaking it as he started to smile and then, to laugh hysterically.

Nancy felt tears stinging her eyes, and she didn't know whether they were tears of happiness or chagrin. Ben had done it — he had won the place in the play-offs for Tarenton. He was no traitor after all.

CHAPTER

"How did he do it?" Pres was standing in the corridor outside the gym, hugging any girl who happened to be within reach. Everyone was laughing and slapping one another on the back. It was almost too good to be true — Tarenton had won the crucial one. They were going to the play-offs and Garrison wasn't.

"I mean, he was brilliant! I've never seen ball played like that!" Walt was jumping around like a nut.

"You won the bet, Pres!" Mary Ellen was delirious. She and Patrick had their arms around each other and, until now, had seemed oblivious to the excitement around them.

"That's right." Patrick nodded. "Which means that you don't owe Vanessa a thing. And she owes *you* fifty dollars!"

"Wasn't my brother terrific?" Angie demanded of Arne, who was sitting on the floor in a doorway beside her. "I mean, Ben and Donny did a great job, but Andrew saved that last basket just before halftime. He was wonderful." Her eyes were bright with pride for her brother.

"You bet," Arne agreed. "I mean, what I know about basketball would fit on the head of a pin, but Andrew looked great out there. To me, anyhow."

Nancy stood apart from the celebrators, stunned and puzzled. Why had he won it? And now, what would happen to him for not throwing the game? In all those gangster movies, if you didn't live up to your dirty promises, you got rubbed out. She didn't want that to happen to him — or anything horrible, for that matter. Ben had done something truly awful, but he didn't deserve to suffer for it now that he'd turned around and done the right thing. He wasn't *that* awful.

Vanessa stormed down the hall, her leather jeans squeaking angrily, her dark hair a storm cloud around her head. Johnny Bainbridge was hurrying after her, a worried look on his face.

"Vannie, wait up! Listen, I can — " he began.

"You can go jump in a lake! I can't believe you could swear Garrison would win and then pull *this* on me."

Vanessa was as angry as Nancy had ever seen her, her nostrils arched and flaring above a quivering mouth, but it didn't phase Nancy in the slightest. She dared to do the unthinkable. She went right up to Vanessa and laughed in her face. Vanessa raised her hand to strike her, and Nancy didn't move. She stood there smiling and dared the other girl to hit her. The other cheerleaders watched anxiously, waiting for the cataclysm, but Pres jumped in just before Vanessa's fingers made contact.

"Don't do it, Van," he warned her.

"That's all right, Pres," Nancy assured him evenly. "She's in enough trouble as it is. Aren't you, Vanessa?"

"I didn't do anything," she sputtered. "It was all him." She pointed at Johnny accusingly. "He offered that weasel a bribe. Was it my fault that Ben didn't take it?"

"He what?" Walt couldn't contain himself. "But it was Donny! I heard him — "

Olivia put a hand over his mouth. "Let her finish, Walt."

"Vanessa." Johnny's former self-confidence had vanished. "Let's not let this thing get out of control, okay? It was just a joke," he told the others nervously.

"Some joke!" Vanessa smirked. "Johnny offered Ben two hundred dollars to lose. And he would have taken it, too, if it hadn't been for *her*." She turned on Nancy with a scathing look, raking her with coal-black eyes that seemed to spit out their evil intention at the world. "He gave it all back right before the game, rolled up the money in a T-shirt and practically threw it in Johnny's lap."

"Boy, you've pulled some rotten ones in your time, Van," Pres commented. "But this is the lowest. You could go to jail for fixing games."

She smiled meanly at him. "Not me. My hands are totally and completely clean. I never chipped in. I only encouraged Johnny to do it so I'd win my bet with you. He's the only guilty party."

"And about that bet, Vanessa. . . ." It was Ben. Everyone turned around at the sound of his voice. "You owe Pres fifty dollars."

"Why, you dirty. . . ." She gritted her teeth, storming over to him with fury that startled the other kids. Ben didn't shrink away but stood his ground. "I'm reporting you both to my father. It seems to me the superintendent of schools will have a lot to say about kids who fix games."

"And what's he going to say about you, Vanessa?" Pres asked calmly. "About daughters who make bets and try to mess up other people's lives?"

Vanessa was silent, suddenly aware of the fact that if she ratted on Johnny and Ben, she, too, might look guilty.

"I think we should all forget it," Ben said. "Let's keep it right where it belongs — among us. Just the eleven of us."

"I agree." Pres came over and stood beside her. "I don't want your money, Van. I'd just like, someday, for you to wake up and not see everybody in the vicinity as your natural enemy. You don't tell and we don't tell — how's that?"

She saw that she was beaten, and she didn't even protest. Solemnly, she turned on her heels and walked away, disappearing through the big metal doors at the end of the corridor. Everyone was silent until she vanished. Then they all started talking again, as though she'd broken their spell and they were now free to be themselves. Johnny started after her, but Ben put a restraining hand on his arm.

"Hey, what are you going to do about that cash? The guys you took it from didn't get what they paid for, so the only logical conclusion is that you have to return it. Right?" He stared the other boy down, demanding an answer.

Johnny scowled at him. "You really won't say anything, Adamson? One word and I could be drummed off the team."

"You could be kicked out of Garrison on your ear," Walt interjected. "But I have a feeling that what we all learned here tonight will go no further than this room — this corridor, I mean."

Ben nodded. "Looks like if you give the money back, you've got a clean slate. Just like me."

The two boys exchanged a look, one that tested the limits of their former friendship. Once they had played ball together; there was no reason why they couldn't play by the rules together.

"You got a deal," Johnny said. Then he walked away abruptly, wanting to get out of Tarenton as fast as he possibly could.

"Well, now that the bad guys are gone," Patrick said, "how about a pizza?" He drew Mary Ellen to him and planted a deliriously happy kiss on her lips.

"My treat," she said when he finally released her. "And I think we should make it a little fancier than pizza. How about dinner at the Manor — on me. I have to do something with that money I inherited." She was completely in her element tonight, at peace with herself and her desires. Right now, at this moment, she would have been content to stay beside Patrick, to remain surrounded by her friends who had spurred her school on to victory. She might not feel the same tomorrow, but for now, it felt good.

"The Manor! What a terrific idea! I like classy places," Walt declared, sweeping Olivia toward the door with a flourish. "Hey, I better apologize to Donny. I was pretty rotten to him."

"You sure were," Olivia agreed. "But since you can't tell him what actually went on, you better think up some pretty terrific excuse. Tomorrow," she added when he started looking very serious. "You coming, Pres? Nancy, we'll meet you in the parking lot."

The seven kids knew enough to leave Nancy and Ben alone. When the corridor was empty, and the echo of feet had died away, the two of them stood staring at each other.

"Well . . ." Nancy began.

"Wait a second. Me first." Ben didn't try to approach her. He kept his distance, sensing that it was too soon to expect her to forgive him. His eyes were softer than she had ever seen them, his hawklike face almost shy. "It's not worth winning if you aren't happy about it, Nancy."

"Don't be silly," she said, not knowing exactly what she felt. "Of course I'm happy. I'm thrilled."

"I should never have taken that money. I could kick myself for even thinking I could. I know you probably won't want to go out with me after this, but you should know that I care about you. If it took losing you for me to realize what a dope I've been, then maybe something good came out of

168

all this. I'm just sorry I couldn't have stopped myself from even agreeing to that stupid deal."

"I am, too." She couldn't take her eyes off him. He seemed to be changing even as she looked at him. He was a nicer person than she'd given him credit for, and he cared about her more than any boy she'd ever dated. But she couldn't shake the worry that he'd *wanted* to cheat — he'd wanted to take money for betraying his school. If you intended to do something bad but didn't, was it as evil as if you went through with it?

"Well, I guess you shouldn't keep the other guys waiting, huh?" He stuck his biker's cap on his head and turned away, hoping the hurt didn't show too much. He was still a tough guy, and liked to think of himself as somebody who could take it all, no matter how bad.

Nancy nodded and started down the hall. She stopped halfway and turned around. "Come with us," she offered quietly.

"You mean it?" His face was shining.

"I don't say things I don't mean."

He came to her, his arms tight at his sides. But as he got closer, he put one hand in his pocket and brought out a little gilt box. "These are yours, Nancy. They could never belong to anyone else. And I've paid for them honestly. I want you to have them."

She took the earrings with a smile. Actually, she'd missed wearing them, because they reminded her of what she and Ben had shared — if only for a brief time. Slowly, she took them out of the box and put them on. "Thank you," she said simply.

He lifted his arms then, and she came to him, entering his embrace with a sigh of relief. She put her head on his chest and he wrapped his arms around her and they just stood there, very still, being quiet together. She looked up into his face, willing whatever might happen between them to happen.

"You don't hate me?" he asked gently.

She shrugged, then grinned. "Not too much."

They both laughed and started running for the door. The other kids were lined up in the parking lot, waiting for them. Patrick had taken a basketball from the gym and was passing it back and forth with Pres, Arne, and Angie. Walt and Olivia were sitting on one of the top steps, their ears practically glued to the door, and Mary Ellen was doing leg lifts to keep warm. Clearly, there had been a lot of discussion about whether or not Nancy was going to come out alone. When they saw her with Ben, a cheer went up.

"Way to go, Adamson!" Pres yelled.

The girls thumped Nancy on the back, and the four guys surrounded them, swooping Ben up in their midst. Then, altogether, they did a little spontaneous dance in the moonlight, celebrating anything and everything: the team's victory, Ben's becoming a good guy, and Nancy's forgiving him. Nancy reached over for Ben's hand and grabbed it, and held it for a second until Patrick threw the basketball right at Ben. He caught it, then passed it to Walt, who dribbled it once and gave it to Olivia. It went the rounds — to Mary Ellen, to Arne, to Angie, to Nancy, to Pres, and back to

Ben again. He chuckled and hoisted the ball high, twirling it expertly on one finger.

"Tonight, Tarenton. Tomorrow, the world!" he proclaimed. The sky was so clear, and the moon was full and bright — as bright as the stars of Tarenton High who had scored so many victories in one brief night.

"Let's hear it for us!" yelled Mary Ellen as she grabbed the ball from Ben and tossed it high in the air. The other kids rallied around her, laughing. Cheating was easy to do, but right now, it was easier to forgive and forget. What the cheerleaders had together was special — too good to spoil — and they knew it. Tonight, at least, they had met their challenge and come through on top.

Who is the strange young man who has been approaching the girls? Read Cheerleaders #12, Staying Together.

Books chosen with you in mind from

—Pass the word.

Living...loving...growing.
That's what **POINT** books are all about!
They're books you'll love reading and
will want to tell your friends about.

Don't miss these other exciting **Point** titles!

NEW POINT TITLES! $2.25 each